A Scientist's Equipment

Name_____

Scientists use many different kinds of special equip..... .....ly. Label the equipment below.

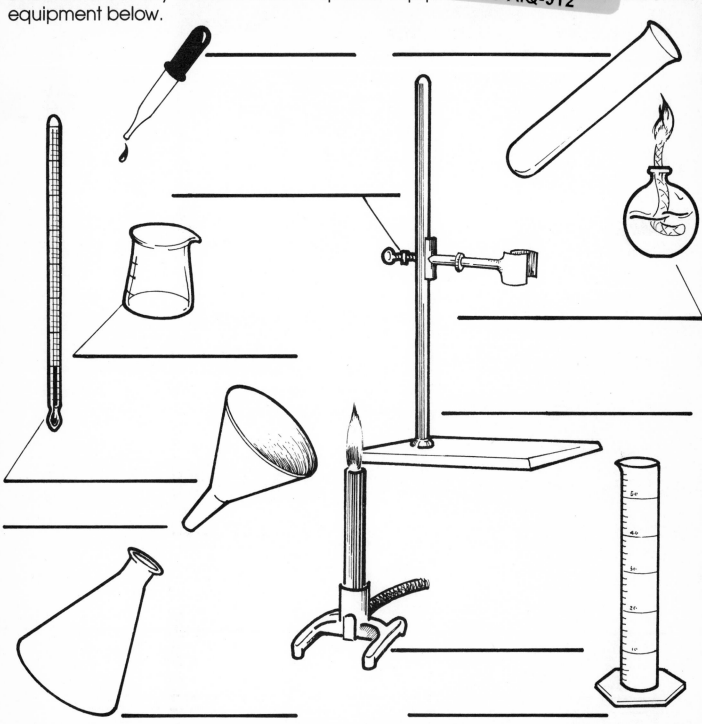

_____

_____

_____

_____

_____

_____

_____

WORD BANK

beaker	ringstand	graduated cylinder
test tube	funnel	dropper
thermometer	flask	test tube clamp
Bunsen burner	alcohol lamp	

How Long Is It?

The meter is the standard unit of measurement when measuring the length of an object or the distance between two objects. Use either <u>kilometer</u>, <u>meter</u>, <u>centimeter</u> or <u>millimeter</u> to label the unit that would be used to measure the objects in the pictures below.

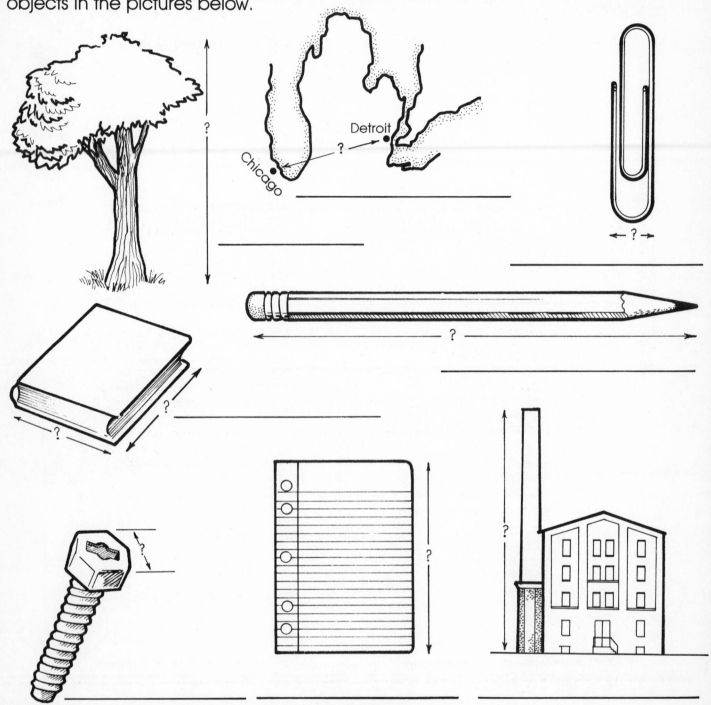

WORD BANK

meter   kilometer   centimeter   millimeter

The Long and Short of It

Name_____

Weight, length, area and volume are properties of matter that scientists can measure. Scientists use the units of grams, meters and liters to measure these properties.

Write the abbreviation for each of these units of measurement.

Unit of Measure	Abbreviation
gram	
kilogram	
milligram	
meter	
kilometer	
centimeter	
millimeter	
square centimeters	
cubic centimeters	
liter	
milliliter	

WORD BANK

g	kg	mg	m	km	cm
mm	cm^2	cm^3	l	ml	

Celsius vs. Fahrenheit

Name_____

The thermometer on this page compares the Celsius and Fahrenheit scales. Label the temperatures on the Celsius and Fahrenheit scales using the temperatures from the **WORD BANK**.

CELSIUS   FAHRENHEIT

____ °C   ____ °F

____ °C   ____ °F

____ °C   ____ °F

____ °C   ____ °F

WORD BANK

0	20	32	37
98.6	100	212	70

4

Balances

The mass of an object can be measured using a balance. Two common types of balances are the triple beam balance and the double pan balance.

Name each balance pictured below and then label the parts. The words in the Word Bank may be used more than once.

Balance: _____

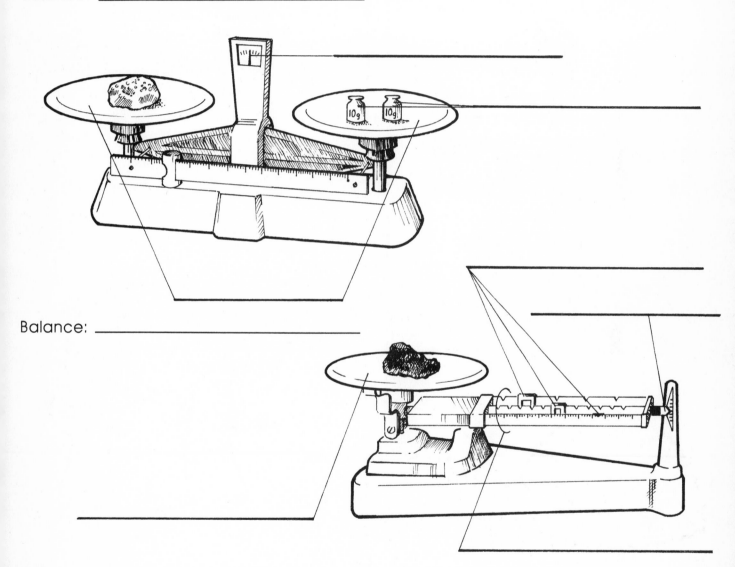

Balance: _____

WORD BANK

pointer	mass (10g each)	beams
pans	riders	pan
triple beam balance	double pan balance	

Reading a Double Pan Balance

Name _____

To determine the weight of an object using a double pan balance, find the sum of masses needed to balance the two pans. Do this by making the pointer on the balance line up with the indicated line.

Find the mass of each of the objects pictured below.

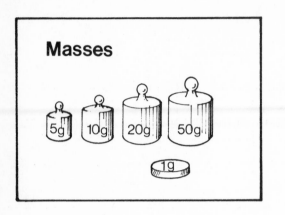

1. _____ g

2. _____ g

3. _____ g

4. _____ g

Reading a Triple Beam Balance

To determine the mass or weight of an object using a triple beam balance, find the sum of the masses shown on all the riders.

Find the mass indicated on each of the triple beam balances pictured below.

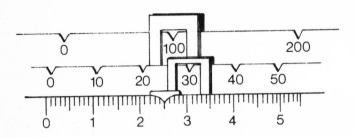

1. _____   4. _____

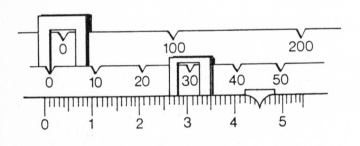

2. _____   5. _____

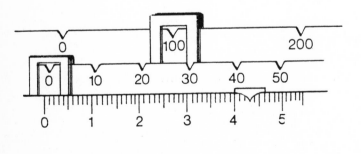

3. _____   6. _____

Reading a Graduated Cylinder

Name _____

Small quantities of a liquid can be measured using a graduated cylinder. You may notice how the liquid curves up the side of the cylinder. To get an accurate reading, read the measurement at the bottom of the curve, or *meniscus*.

Read the following volumes.

1. _____ ml

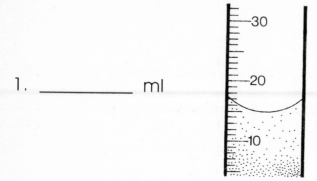

5. _____ ml

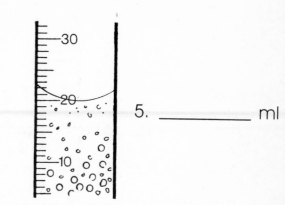

2. _____ ml

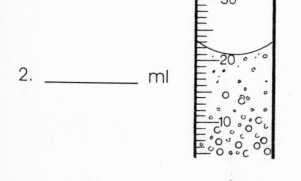

6. _____ ml

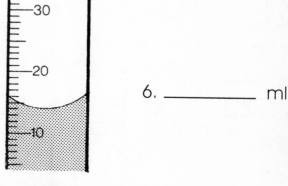

3. _____ ml

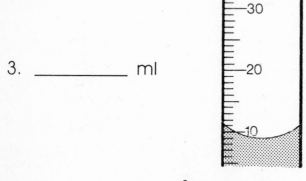

7. _____ ml

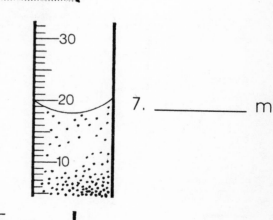

4. _____ ml

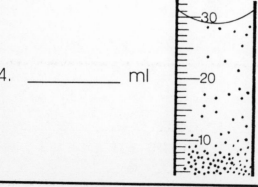

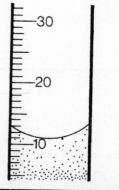

8. _____ ml

Chemical Symbols

Use the symbols to find the names of the elements needed to complete the puzzle.

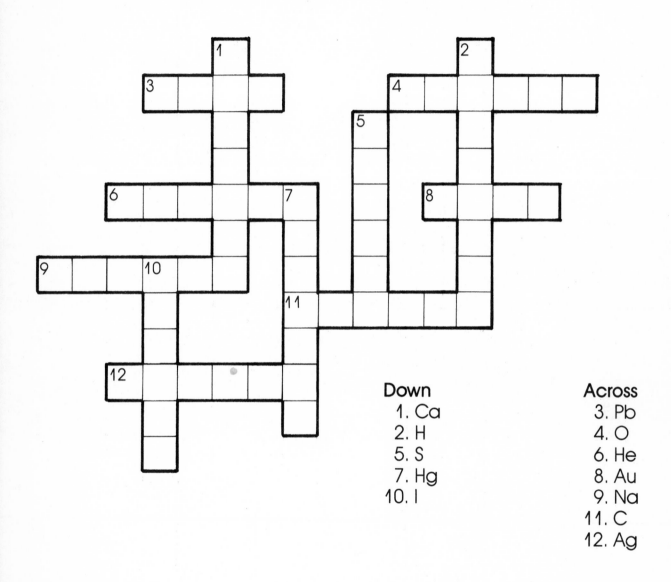

Down
1. Ca
2. H
5. S
7. Hg
10. I

Across
3. Pb
4. O
6. He
8. Au
9. Na
11. C
12. Ag

WORD BANK

lead	oxygen	helium	gold
sodium	carbon	silver	iodine
calcium	mercury	sulfur	hydrogen

9

Periodic Table of Elements

Name_____

The periodic table can give you a lot of information about each of the elements. Use the **WORD BANK** to label the type of information that the symbols, names and letters represent for each of the elements.

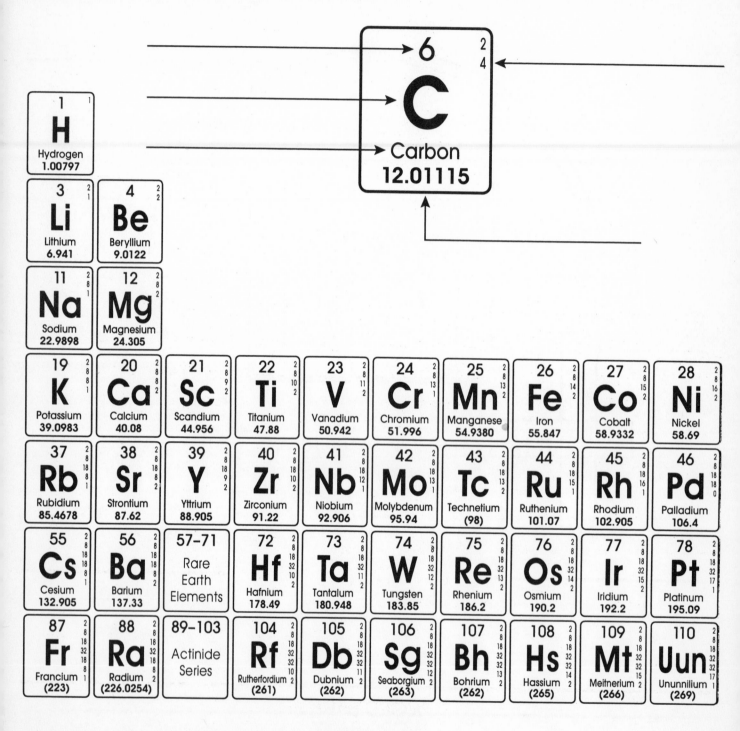

Word Bank

atomic number
atomic mass

element's symbol
element's name

electrons in outer shell

Atoms

Label the parts of the helium atom pictured below.

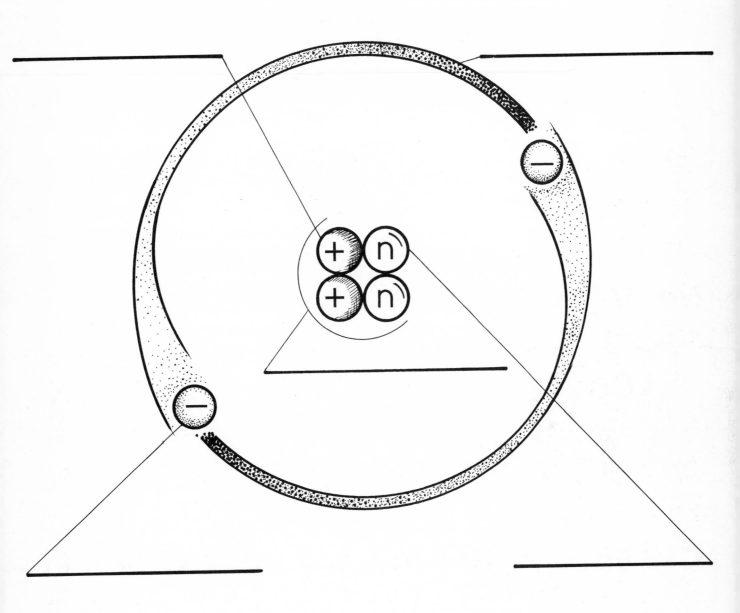

_____

_____

_____

_____

WORD BANK

proton   nucleus   neutron
orbit (shell)   electron

11

Protons, Neutrons and Electrons

Name_____

The atomic number of an atom is the number of protons in each atom of that element. Because atoms are electrically neutral, the atomic number is also the number of electrons. The atomic mass tells the number of protons and neutrons in an atom. By subtracting the atomic number from the atomic mass you can find the number of neutrons.

Complete the chart below.

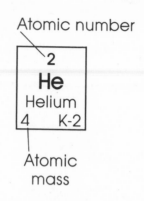

HELIUM ATOM

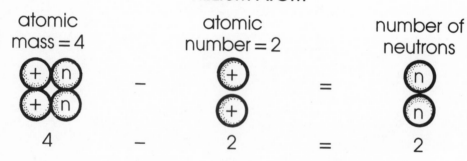

ELEMENT	SYMBOL	ATOMIC NUMBER	ATOMIC MASS	PROTONS	NEUTRONS	ELECTRONS
helium	He	2	4			
nitrogen	N	7	14			7
carbon	C	6	12			
sodium	Na	11	23			
iron	Fe	26			30	
copper	Cu		64	29		
silver	Ag	47	108		61	

Name That Molecule!

Write the chemical formula for each molecule pictured below.

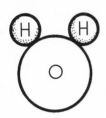

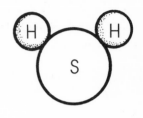

_____

_____

_____

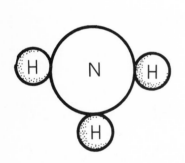

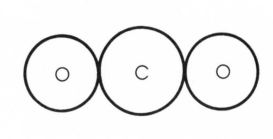

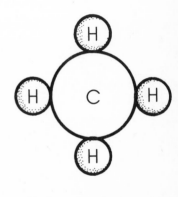

_____

_____

_____

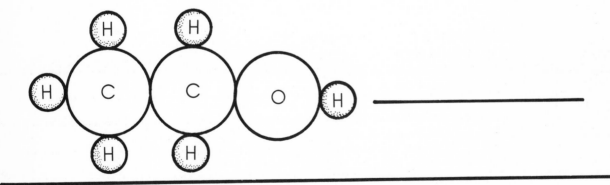 _____

_____

WORD BANK

H_2O CH_4 H_2S Fe_2O_3

C_2H_5OH CO_2 NH_3

Chemical Formulas

Name_____

A chemical formula is a shorthand way to write the name of a compound. Complete the chart below for each of the formulas.

	Compound	Formula	Elements
1.		NaCl	
2.		HCl	
3.		NaOH	
4.		H_2O	
5.		CO_2	
6.		H_2SO_4	
7.		$CuSO_4$	
8.		C_2H_5OH	

WORD BANK

sodium chloride
water
sulfuric acid
sodium
copper

hydrochloric acid
oxygen
copper sulfate
chlorine
sulfur

sodium hydroxide
carbon dioxide
alcohol
hydrogen
carbon

Chemicals

Name _____

Use what you have learned about chemicals to complete this puzzle. You may need to refer to your science book or encyclopedia.

Across

1. A substance that contains two or more chemical elements.
3. A simple substance made of one type of atom.
7. The smallest particle that displays the physical and chemical properties of a compound.
8. A negatively-charged particle that orbits the nucleus of an atom.
9. What everything is made of; the smallest unit of an element.

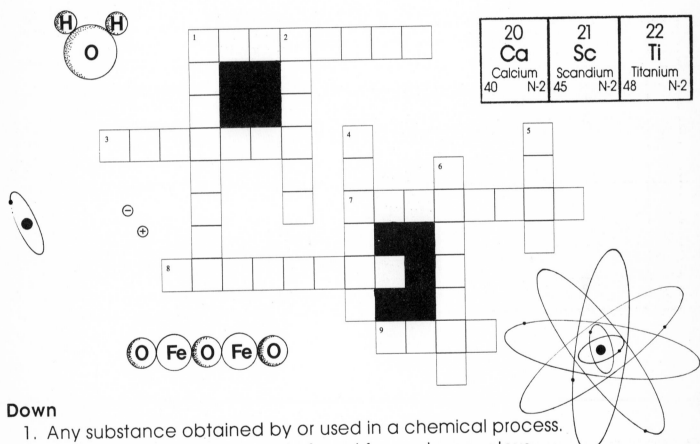

Down

1. Any substance obtained by or used in a chemical process.
2. A positively-charged particle found free or in a nucleus.
4. It stands for the name of an element.
5. **Au** is the symbol for _____ .
6. A particle in an atom or by itself with no electrical charge.

WORD BANK

compound	proton	symbol	neutron	chemical
electron	atom	element	gold	molecule

15

Dry Cells

Name _____

The dry cell is a source of portable power used in flashlights, toys, and radios. There are three basic kinds of dry cells that are commonly used—carbon-zinc, alkaline, and mercury.

Label the parts of this carbon-zinc dry cell illustration.

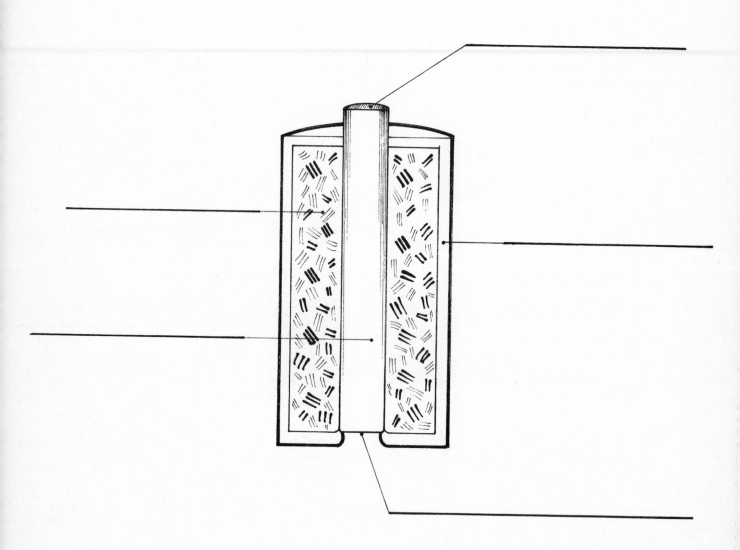

WORD BANK

positive terminal   zinc container   chemical paste
negative terminal   carbon rod

Light Bulb

Label the parts of the incandescent light bulb pictured below.

WORD BANK

bulb   filaments   base   contact

glass support   connecting and supporting wires

Circuits and Switches

To be useful electricity must flow in a circuit. Electric circuits can be illustrated with the help of symbols.

Identify the symbols shown here.

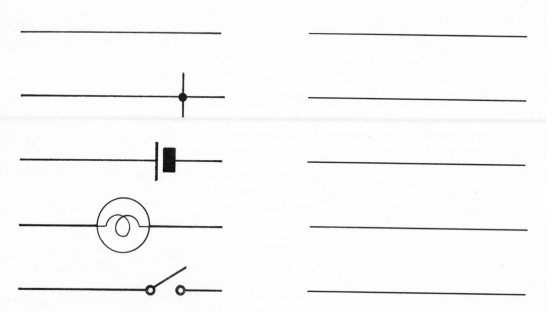

_____   _____

_____   _____

_____   _____

Name each circuit pictured below.

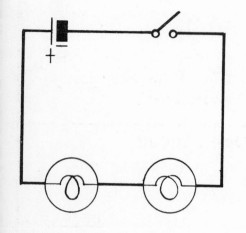   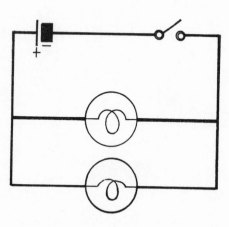   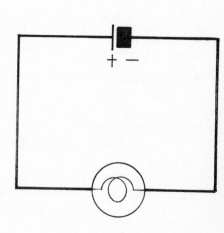

_____   _____   _____

WORD BANK

wire	battery	simple circuit
connection	light bulb	series circuit
switch	parallel circuit	

18

Drawing Electrical Circuits

There are three types of simple electrical circuits: a closed circuit, a parallel circuit, and a series circuit. Each type can be set up in more than one way.

Draw lines to show where the wires should connect to make the following circuits.

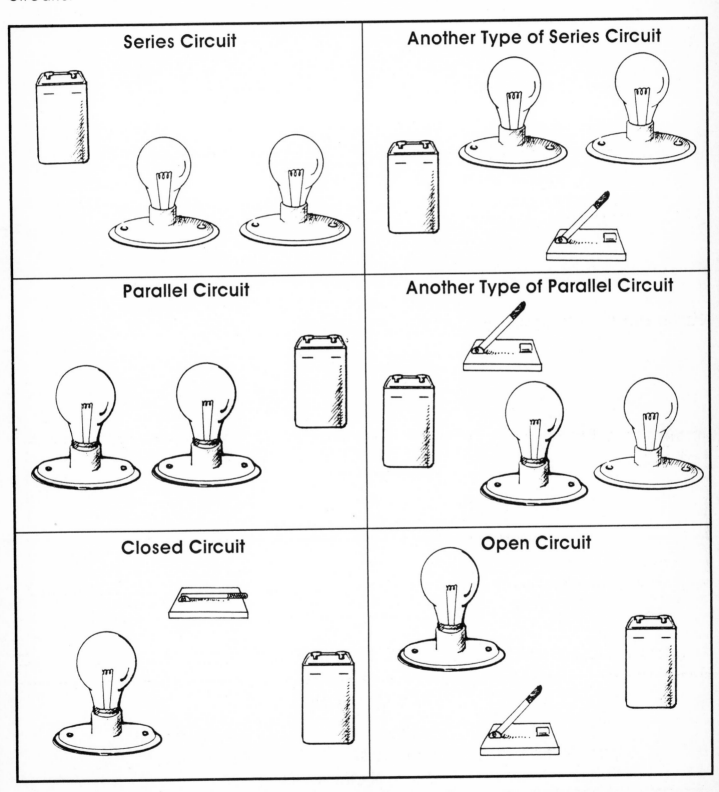

Series Circuit	Another Type of Series Circuit
Parallel Circuit	Another Type of Parallel Circuit
Closed Circuit	Open Circuit

Classy Levers

Name_____

Three classes of levers are pictured below. Label each class of lever and the three lever parts.

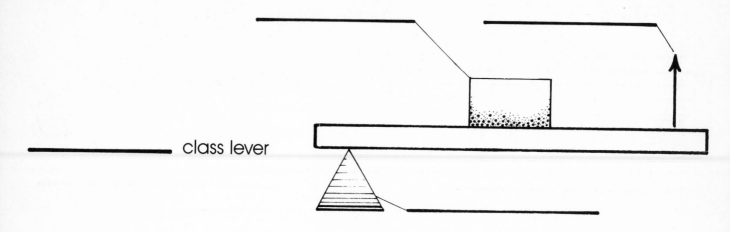

_____ class lever

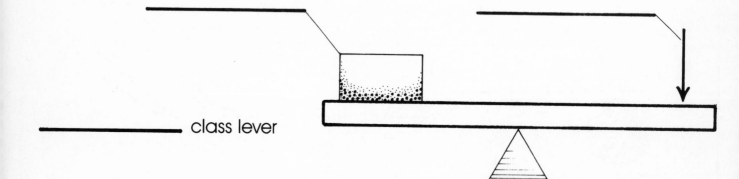

_____ class lever

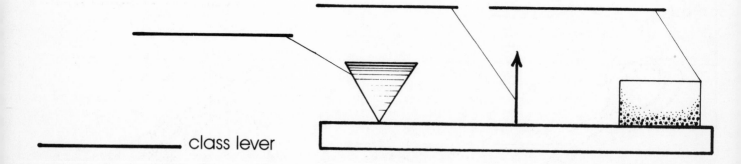

_____ class lever

WORD BANK

first   second   third
load   force   fulcrum

Practical Levers

In the space under each picture below write <u>first</u>, <u>second</u> or <u>third</u> to tell the class of the lever.

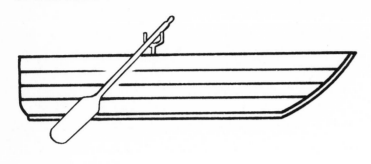

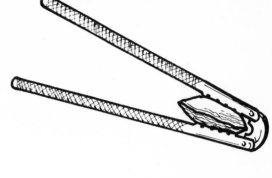

_____

_____

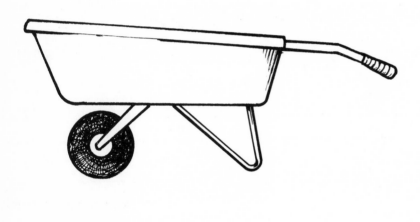

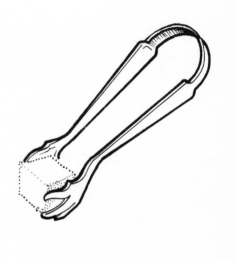

_____

_____

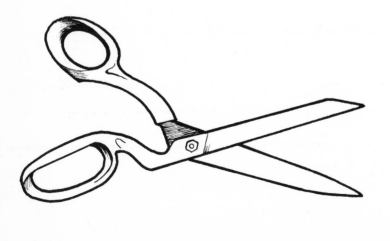

_____

_____

21

Special Inclined Planes

Name_____

Some simple machines are pictured below. Some of these simple machines are special inclined planes, called wedges and screws. Put an "X" on the simple machines that are not special inclined planes. Label the special inclined planes either <u>screw</u> or <u>wedge</u>.

Pedal Power

Name_____

Your bicycle is a combination of many simple machines. Study the bicycle on this page. Circle and label as many simple machines that you can find on the bicycle shown.

WORD BANK

lever   wheel and axle   inclined plane (screw)

Compound Machines

Often two or more simple machines are combined to make one machine called a compound machine. Name the simple machines that are combined to make each of the compound machines pictured below.

_____   _____

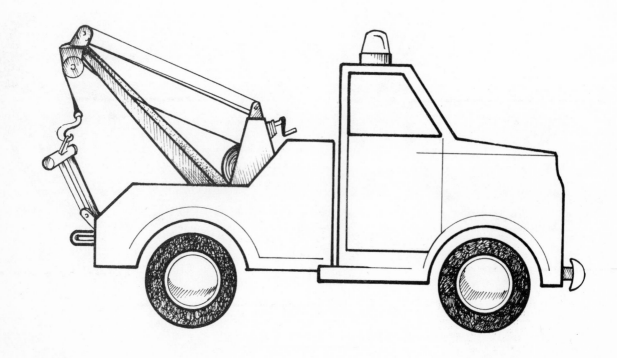

_____

WORD BANK

wheel and axle   inclined plane (wedge, screw)   pulley
lever

24

The Seasons

The diagram below shows the Earth's position in its orbit on four different dates. On the solid line label the equinox dates. On the dotted lines name the season for the Northern Hemisphere.

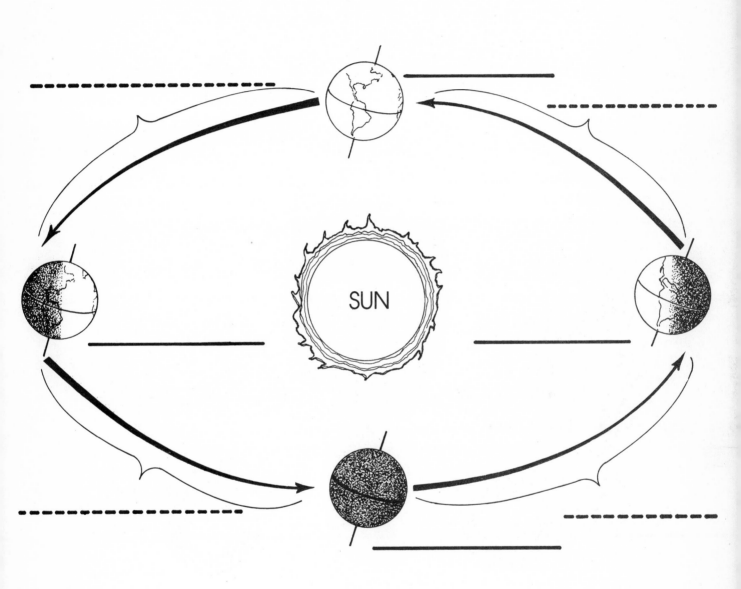

WORD BANK

March 21	December 22	spring	fall
September 22	June 21	winter	summer

Summer and Winter

Name_____

The illustration below shows the Earth's position in relation to the Sun for the summer and winter in the Northern Hemisphere. Label the seasons for the Northern Hemisphere, and name the imaginary lines of latitude on the Earth.

WORD BANK

summer	winter
Arctic Circle	Antarctic Circle
Tropic of Capricorn	Tropic of Cancer
Equator	

Day and Night

Day and night are the result of the Earth's rotation on its axis. Use the words from the **WORD BANK** to label the illustration below.

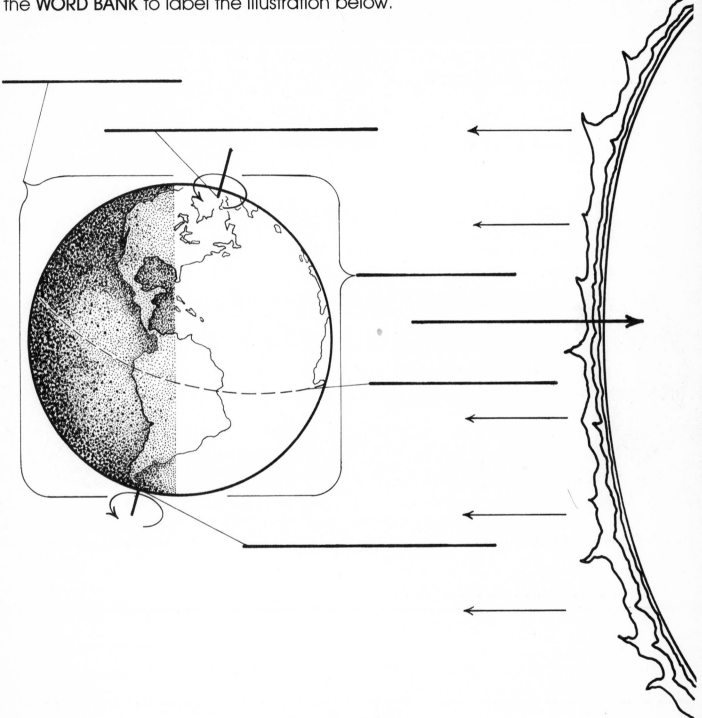

WORD BANK

North Pole	South Pole
day	sun
Equator	night

High Tide

Name_____

The ocean tides are caused mostly by the moon's gravity. When the Sun, moon and Earth line up, the gravitational pull is greatest causing the highest tides, the spring tides. The lowest tides, neap tides, occur when the sun, Earth and moon form right angles. Label the neap tides, spring tides, sun, Earth and moon.

_____ tides

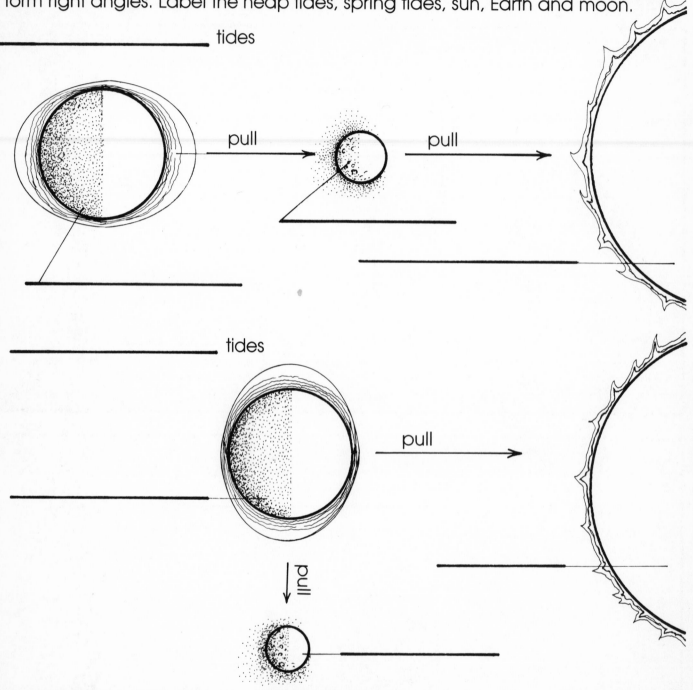

_____ tides

WORD BANK

neap tides	spring tides	sun
moon	Earth	

Space Shadows

When the sun, moon and Earth are in the proper alignment, either the moon can cast a shadow on the Earth, or the Earth can cast a shadow on the moon. Draw the position of the moon and the shadows for both a lunar and solar eclipse. Label the type of eclipse.

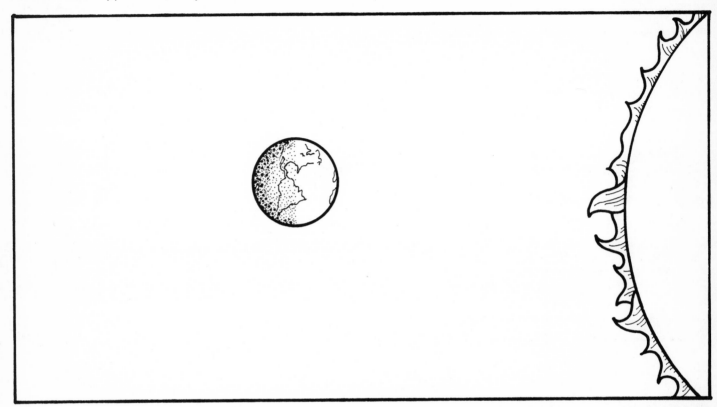

Earth Shadow

When the sun, Earth and moon are in direct line, the moon moves into the Earth's shadow causing a <u>lunar eclipse.</u> Label the orbits and bodies in the illustration below.

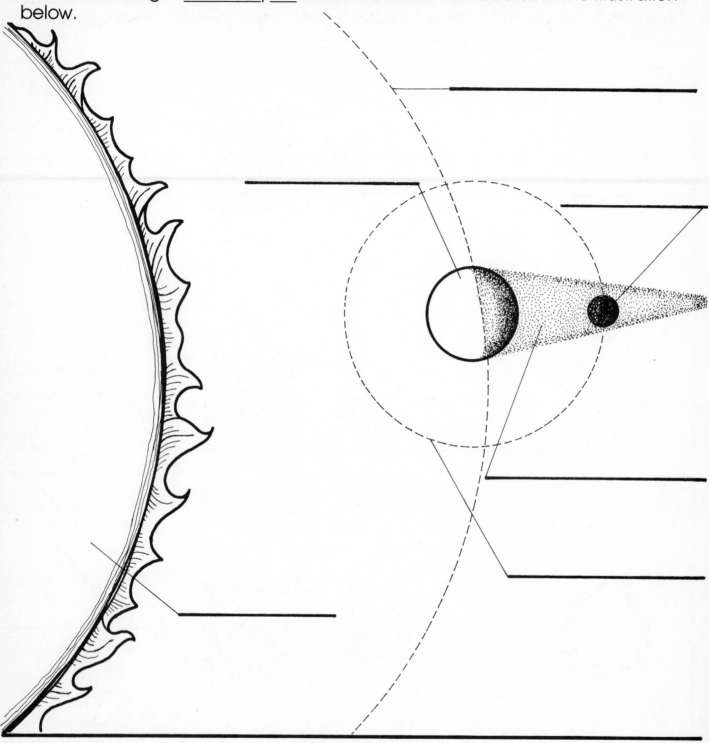

WORD BANK

Earth orbit	moon orbit	moon
Earth	sun	Earth's shadow

     30

Moon Shadows

When the new moon is directly between the Earth and the sun, an eclipse of the sun occurs. The type of <u>solar eclipse</u> that occurs depends on how much sunlight the moon blocks from the view on Earth. Label the three kinds of solar eclipse. Label the moon, sun and Earth.

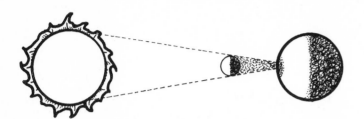  _____

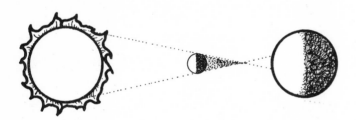  _____

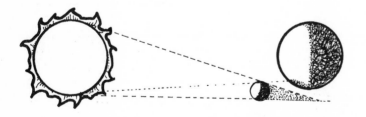  _____

WORD BANK

| total eclipse | annular eclipse | partial eclipse |
| sun | moon | Earth |

Changing Faces

Name_____

As the moon revolves around the Earth, we can see different amounts of the moon's lighted part. Study the drawing of the moon's different phases and each phase as it would be seen from the Earth. Label each phase.

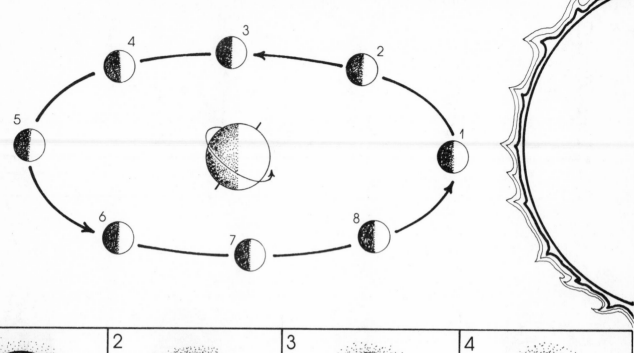

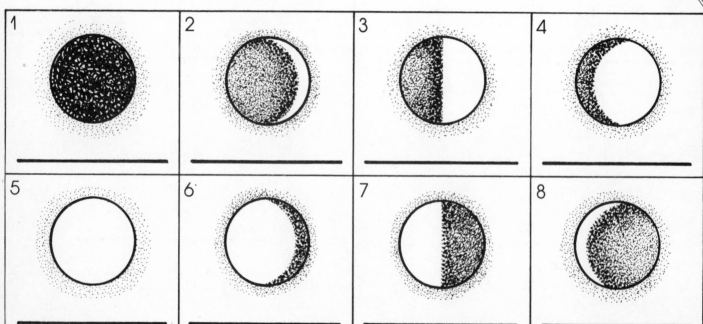

WORD BANK

new moon   waxing crescent   first quarter

waxing gibbous   full moon   waning gibbous

last quarter   waning crescent

Waning and Waxing Moon

Use the **WORD BANK** to label the different phases of the moon.

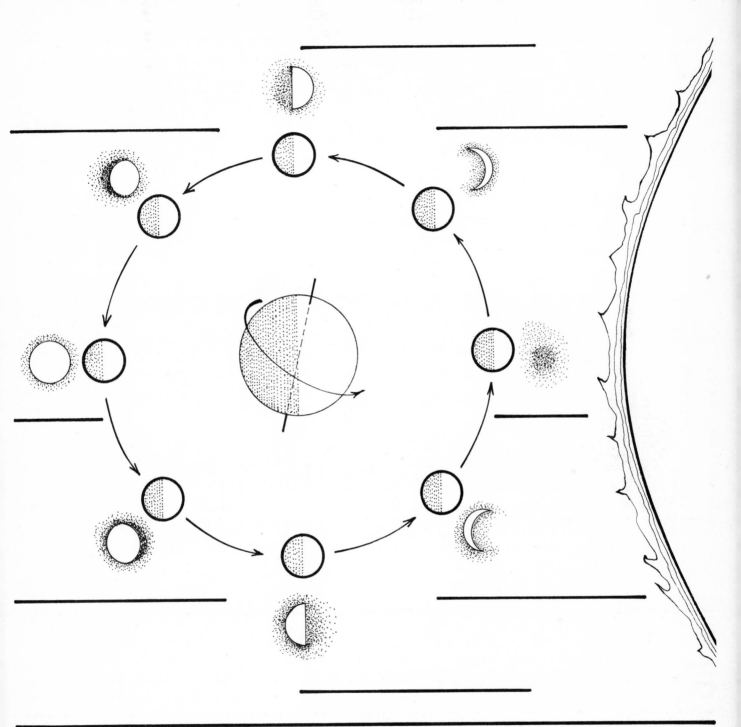

WORD BANK

new   waxing crescent   first quarter
waxing gibbous   full   waning gibbous
last quarter   waning crescent

Planets of the Solar System

All of the planets of the Solar System travel around the sun. Label the planets.

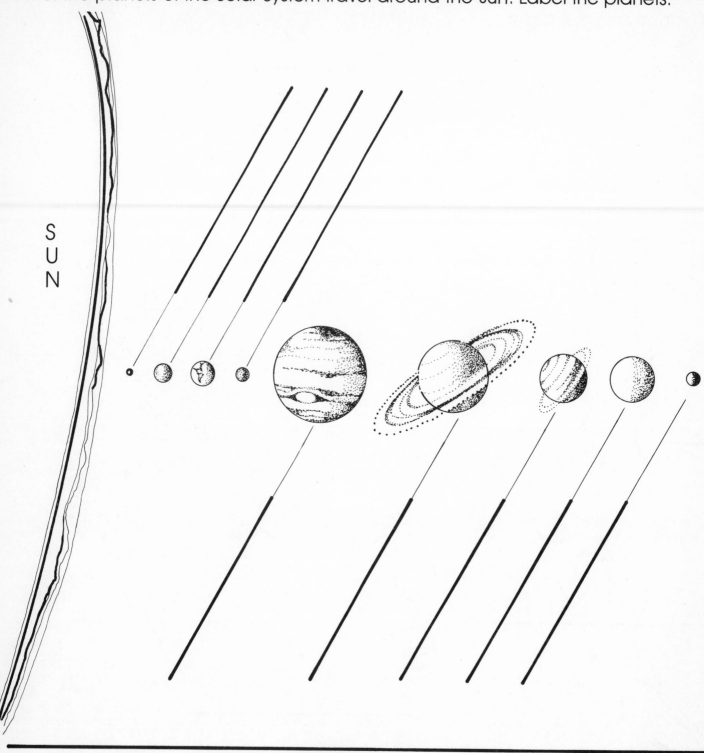

S
U
N

WORD BANK

Mercury	Venus	Earth
Mars	Jupiter	Saturn
Uranus	Neptune	Pluto

The Inner Planets

The planets that are closest to the sun are called the Inner Planets. Label the Inner Planets and the sun.

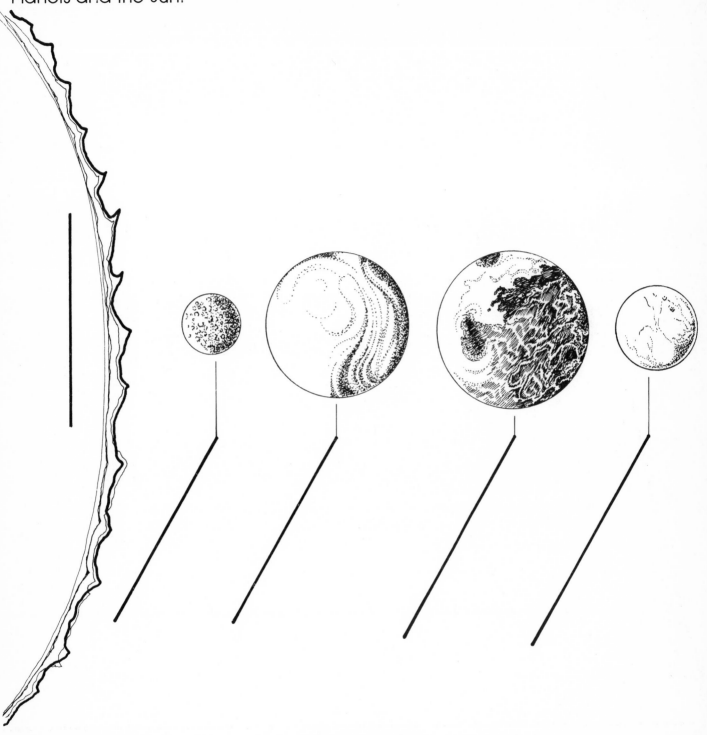

WORD BANK

sun	Venus	Mercury
Earth	Mars	

The Outer Planets

The planets that are farthest from the sun are called the Outer Planets. Label the Outer Planets.

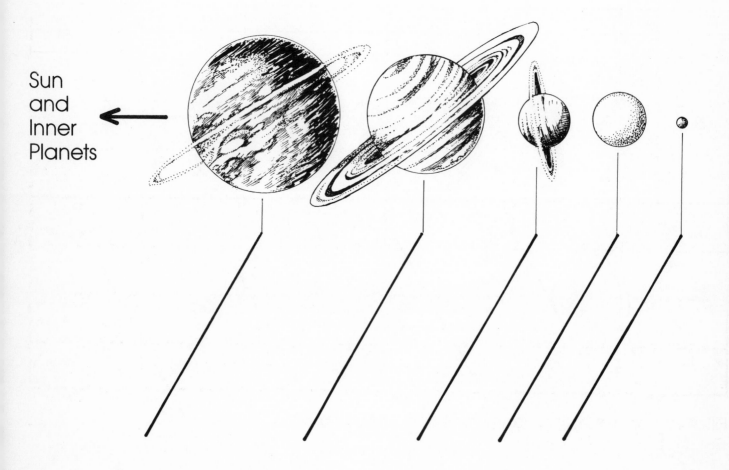

Sun
and
Inner
Planets

WORD BANK

Jupiter   Saturn   Uranus
Neptune   Pluto

Exploring Our Solar System

Name _____

Comets, asteroids, and some meteors travel around the sun in our solar system. But the largest objects traveling around the sun are the planets. Use your science book, encyclopedia, or another source to complete the chart about the planets of our solar system.

Planet	Position From the Sun	Revolution Time (Length of Year — Earth Days)	Rotation Time	Known Satellites	Distance From the Sun

Fill in the names of the planets where they belong.

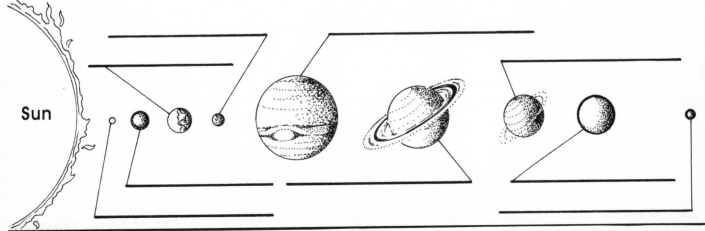

Sun

Puzzling Planets

Name _____

Use what you have learned about the planets of our solar system to complete the puzzle. You may need to refer to your science book or an encyclopedia.

Across

3. I am the closest in size to the Earth.
4. I am the smallest planet.
6. I have the greatest number of natural satellites.
7. I am the only planet known to support life.
8. I am the Red Planet.
9. I am the most distant planet that can be seen without a telescope.

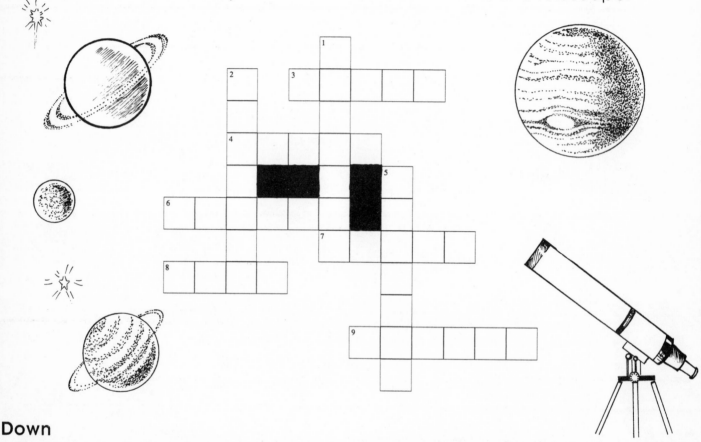

Down

1. I am usually the 8th planet from the Sun, but every 248 years I move inside Pluto's orbit for 20 years.
2. I am a large planet known for my "Great Red Spot."
5. I am the closest planet to the Sun.

WORD BANK

Mercury	Venus	Earth
Mars	Jupiter	Saturn
Uranus	Neptune	Pluto

Our Closest Star–The Sun

The sun is the closest star to the Earth. Use the **WORD BANK** to label the different layers and features of the sun.

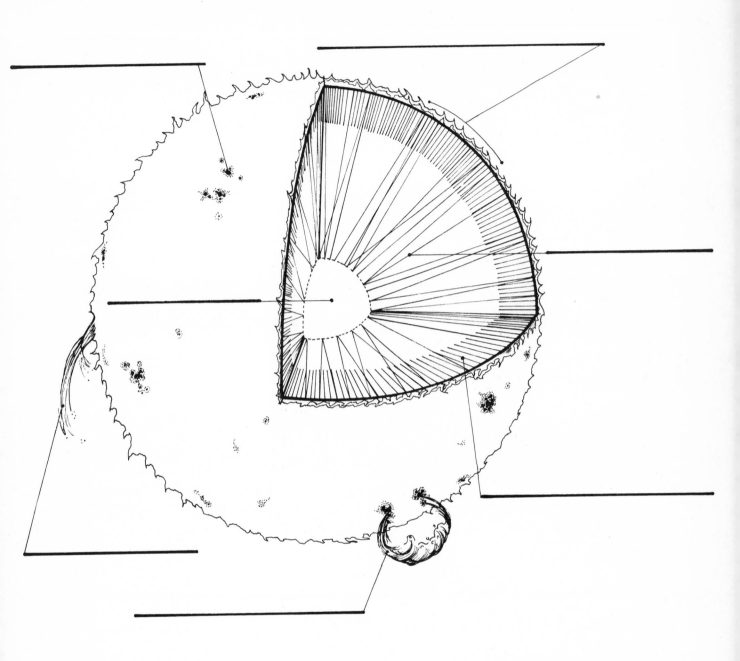

WORD BANK

core   radiative zone

photosphere   chromosphere

flare   sunspot   prominence

39

Dirty Snowballs

Comets are like "dirty snowballs." Use the words from the **WORD BANK** to label the parts of these frozen masses of gas and dust particles.

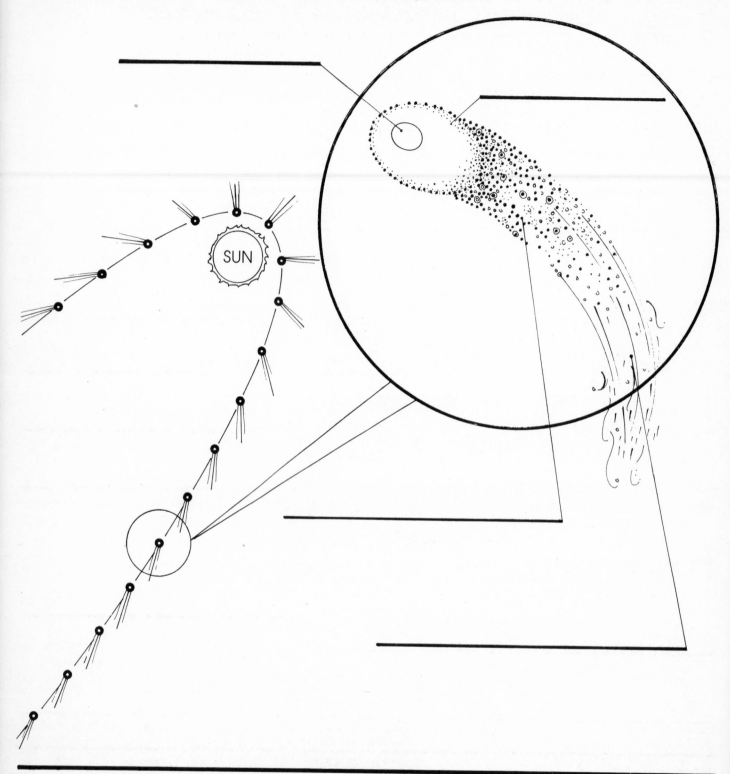

WORD BANK

nucleus   coma   gas tail   dust tail

40

The Asteroid Belt

Scientists believe that asteroids may be pieces of a planet that was torn apart millions of years ago. Thousands of large asteroids have been tracked, but hundreds of thousands of smaller asteroids are in the asteroid belt.
Label the asteroid belt and the planets in the illustration below.

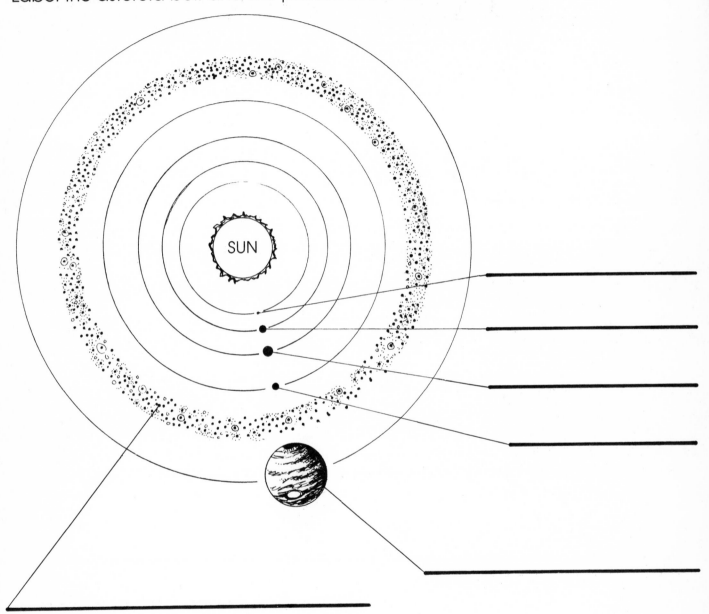

WORD BANK

Mercury	Venus	Earth
Mars	Jupiter	asteroid belt

The North Star

Because the Earth rotates, all the stars in the sky appear to move from east to west. Because Polaris is directly above the North Pole it does not move, and so it is also called the North Star.

Polaris is found in the constellation Ursa Minor, also called the Little Dipper. The Big Dipper is found in the constellation Ursa Major, also called the Great Bear. Trace the Big Dipper and Little Dipper. Label Polaris.

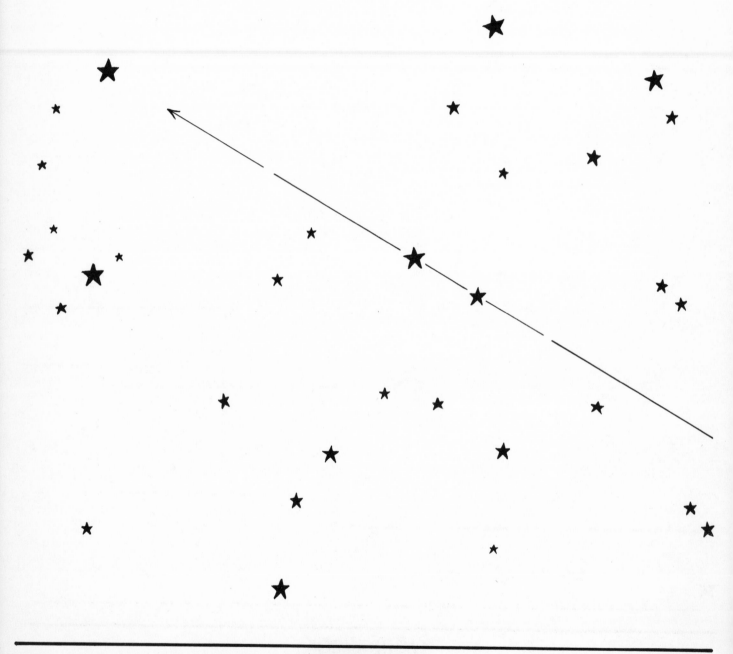

WORD BANK

Big Dipper   Little Dipper   Polaris

42

Pictures in the Night Sky

Name _____

For thousands of years people from every culture have gazed into the night sky and imagined groups of stars outlining a picture. These star pictures, called **constellations**, are like giant dot-to-dot puzzles in the night sky.

Name these well-known constellations.

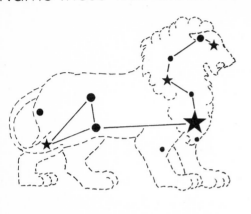

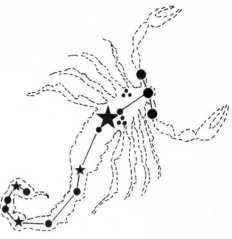

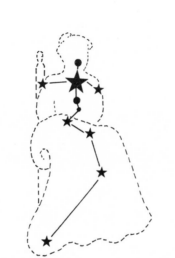

_____

_____

_____

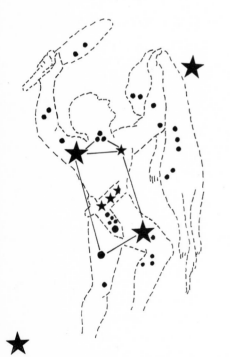

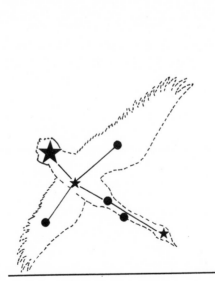

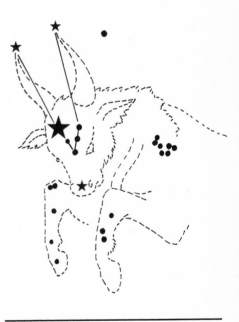

_____

_____

_____

WORD BANK

Orion   Cygnus   Leo

Scorpio   Taurus   Cassiopeia

Galaxies

Name_____

Beyond our galaxy lie billions of other galaxies. Use the **WORD BANK** to label the shapes of some of these galaxies.

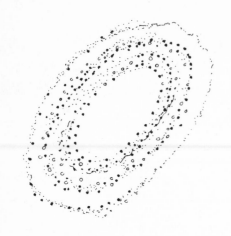

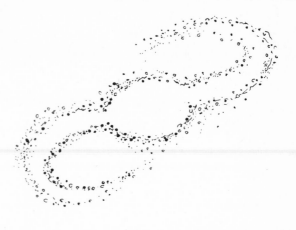

_____

_____

_____

_____

WORD BANK

elliptical   spiral   barred spiral   irregular

Radio Telescope

Name_____

Radio telescopes give us much information about the universe that other kinds of telescopes can't give. Label the parts of the radio telescope.

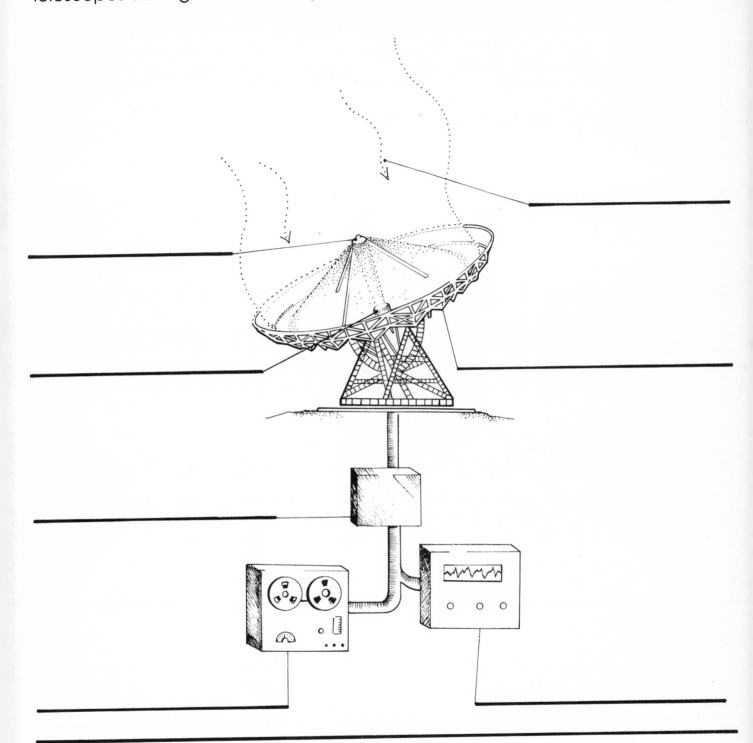

WORD BANK

receiver	reflector dish	vertex box	radio waves
computer	control unit	display unit	

"Optic Glass"

Name_____

In 1609 the Italian astronomer, Galileo, was the first person to see the heavenly bodies closer than they really were with his "optic glass," or telescope. Label the refractor and reflector telescopes and their parts. Use the words from the **WORD BANK**. You may have to use some of the words more than one time.

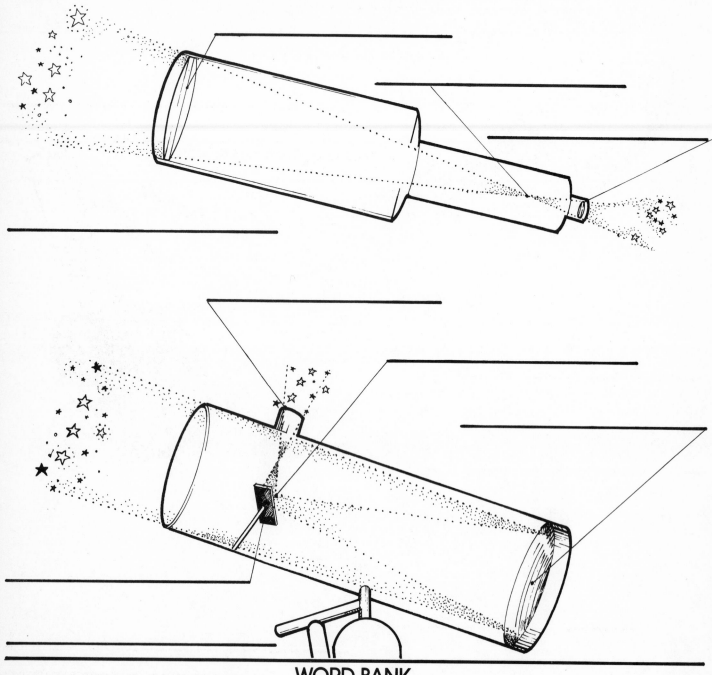

WORD BANK

reflector telescope   refractor telescope
objective lens   eyepiece lens
focal point   flat mirror
objective mirror

The Space Shuttle

Use the words in the **WORD BANK** to label the parts of the Space Shuttle.

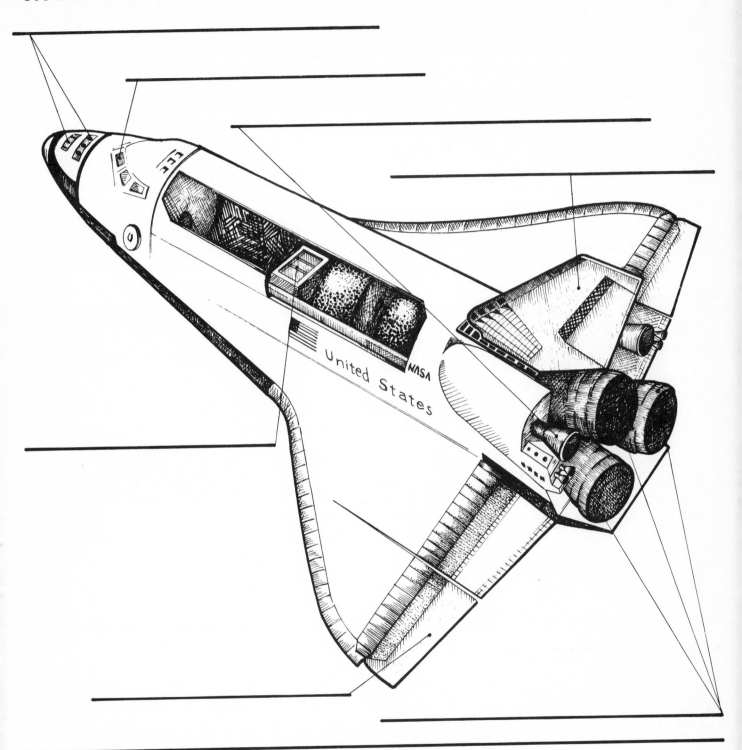

WORD BANK

payload bay   main engines   rudder and speed brake
cockpit   elevon   reaction control jets
orbital maneuvering system engine

The Flight of the Space Shuttle

Name_____

Label the different phases of the Space Shuttle's mission.

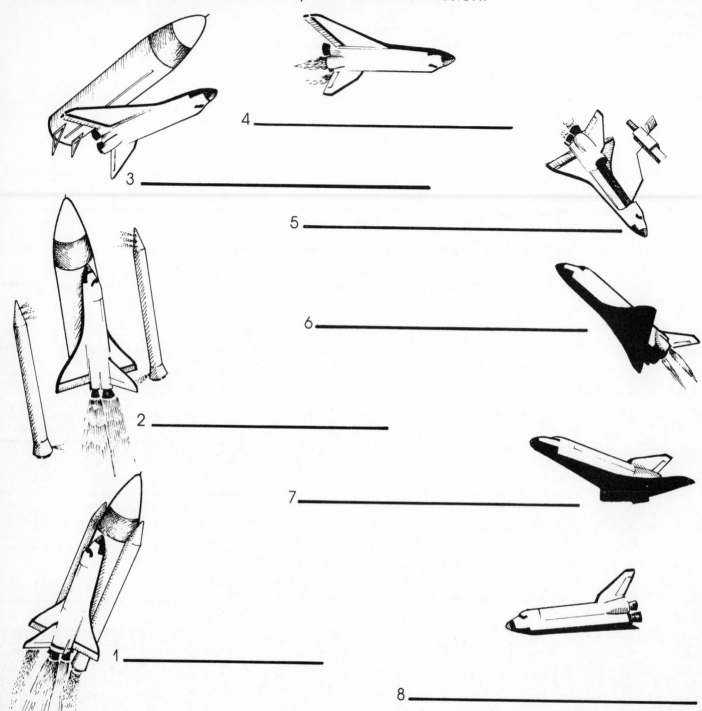

3 _____

4 _____

5 _____

6 _____

2 _____

7 _____

1 _____

8 _____

WORD BANK

orbital activities   landing
reentry   solid rocket booster separation
deorbit   ascent
orbit insertion   external tank separation

Space Shuttle Launch Site

Name_____

Label the parts of the Space Shuttle's launch site using the words from the **WORD BANK.**

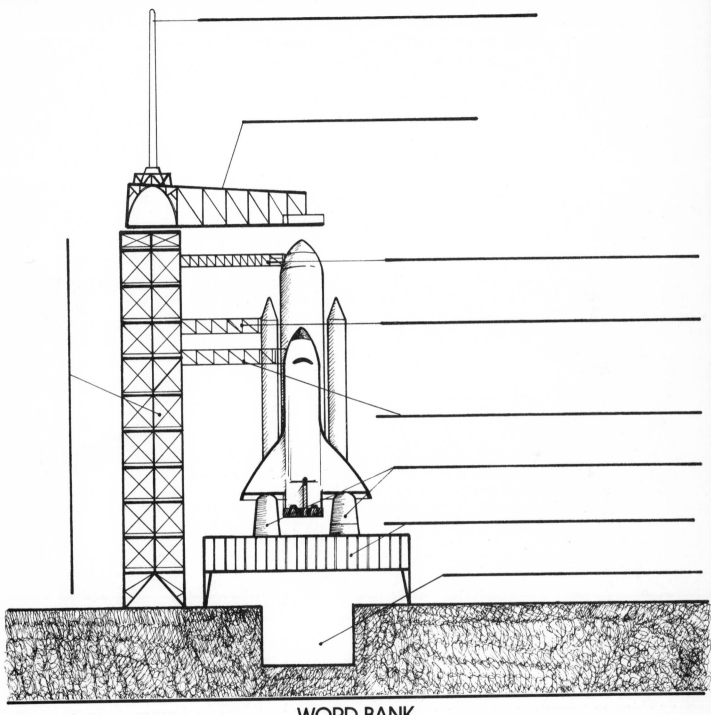

WORD BANK

lightning mast	crane	flame platform
service structure	orbiter access arm	hydrogen venting arm
tail service masts	launching pad platform	oxygen venting arm

Hemispheres

The Earth is a giant sphere. When the Earth is divided into two equal parts each part is called a hemisphere. Label the four hemispheres pictured below using the words from the **WORD BANK.**

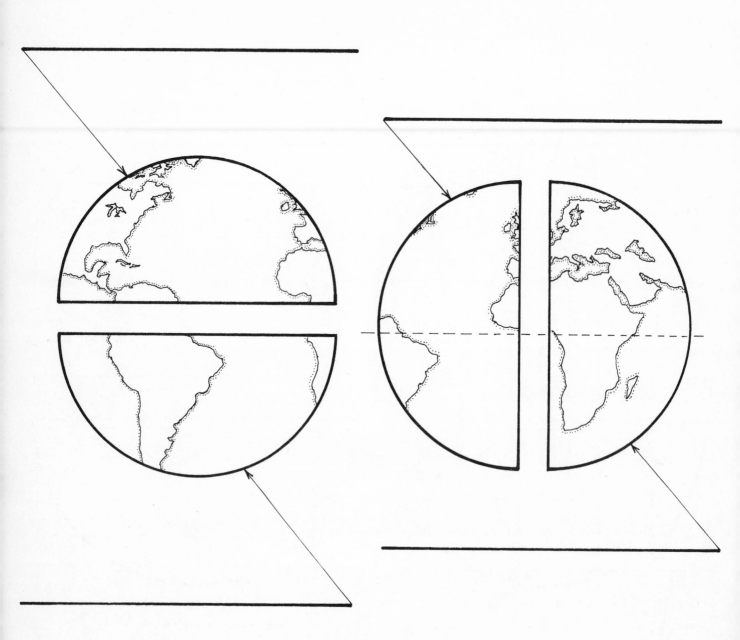

WORD BANK

Northern Hemisphere   Southern Hemisphere
Eastern Hemisphere   Western Hemisphere

More Than One Hemisphere

Name_____

You live in more than one hemisphere. Although it's impossible to live in the Northern and Southern Hemispheres, or the Eastern and Western Hemisphere at the same time, it is possible to live in the Northern and Eastern, or Northern and Western, or Southern and Eastern, or Southern and Western Hemisphere. Label the two hemispheres pictured in each hemisphere.

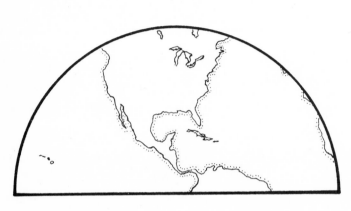

_____ and
_____ Hemispheres

_____ and
_____ Hemispheres

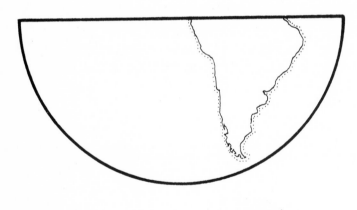

_____ and
_____ Hemispheres

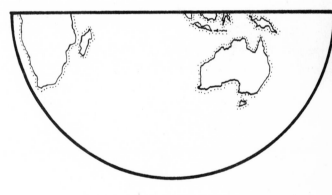

_____ and
_____ Hemispheres

WORD BANK

Northern	Southern
Eastern	Western

Map Features

Name _____

Everyone from the weather forecaster to a family on vacation finds maps as very valuable tools. But they are useful only if you know how to use their many features. Label the parts of the map below. Then explain the purpose of each.

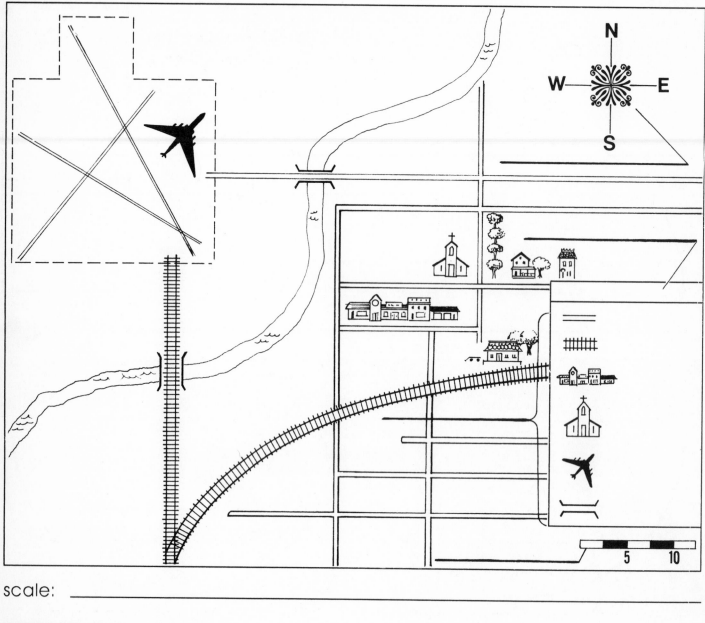

scale: _____

compass rose: _____

map key: _____

symbols: _____

WORD BANK

scale   compass rose   map key   symbols

Using Latitude and Longitude

Name _____

Use the latitude and longitude grid to pinpoint each location specified in the questions below.

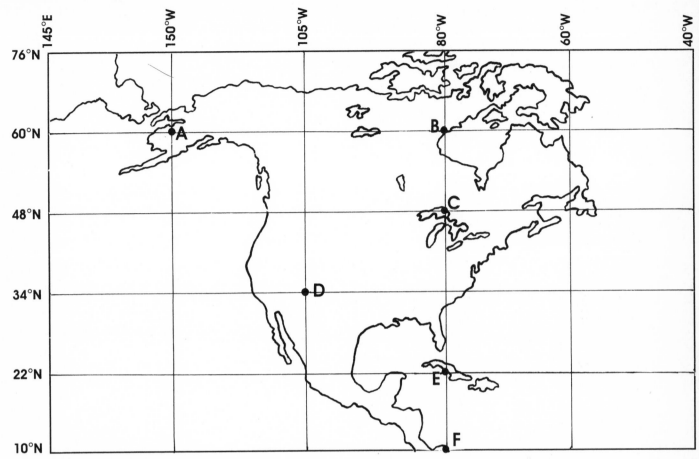

1. What is the latitude of . . .

point **A**? _____   point **D**? _____

point **B**? _____   point **E**? _____

point **C**? _____   point **F**? _____

2. What is the longitude of . . .

point **A**? _____   point **D**? _____

point **B**? _____   point **E**? _____

point **C**? _____   point **F**? _____

3. Give the location of . . .

point **A**. _____   point **D**. _____

point **B**. _____   point **E**. _____

point **C**. _____   point **F**. _____

Sea of Air

Our atmosphere extends several hundred kilometers upward. In the illustration below notice different layers of the atmosphere and what may be found in those layers. Label each of the layers and objects found in these layers using the words from the **WORD BANK.**

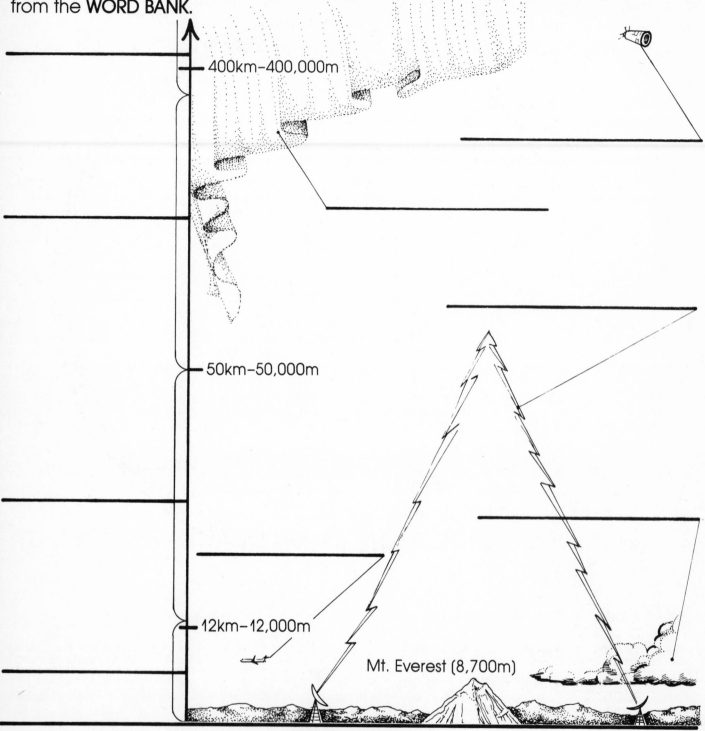

400km–400,000m

50km–50,000m

12km–12,000m

Mt. Everest (8,700m)

WORD BANK

troposphere	stratosphere	ionosphere	radio wave
exosphere	space capsule	aurorae	highest clouds
jet airlines			

54

The Center of the Earth

The Earth has four layers. Color the layers of the Earth and the key.

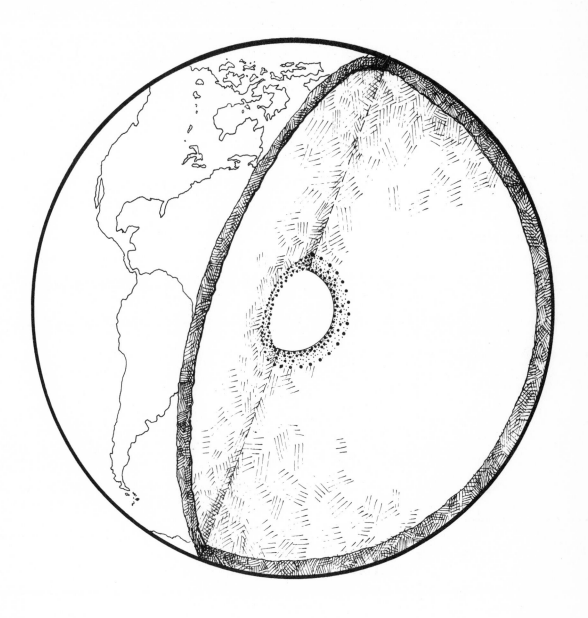

blue	WATER
green	LAND
brown	CRUST (5-70 km thick)
orange	MANTLE (3,000 km thick)
yellow	OUTER CORE (2,000 km thick)
red	INNER CORE (1,500 km thick)

Solid to the Core

If you could take a slice out of the Earth you would find that it has four layers.
Label each of these layers.

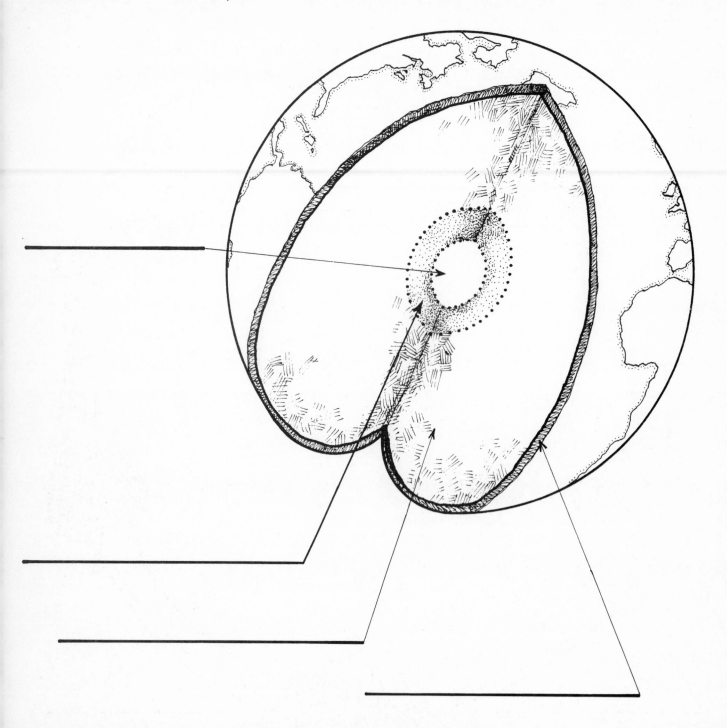

WORD BANK

crust   mantle   outer core
inner core

The Rock Cycle

With the help of heat, pressure, and weathering, one kind of rock can be changed into a new kind of rock. For example, beautiful marble is formed from limestone, and slate comes from shale and clay.

The changing of rocks is an ongoing cycle. There is no true beginning, but it might be easier to understand by beginning with magma. Complete the rock cycle diagram pictured below.

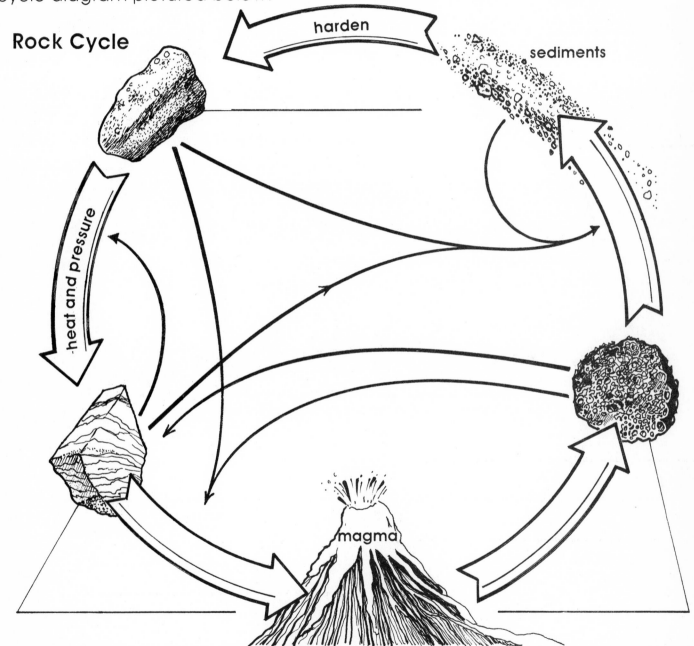

Rock Cycle

harden

sediments

heat and pressure

magma

WORD BANK

sedimentary rock   igneous rock   metamorphic rock
melting   weathering   cooling and hardening

Soil Profile

Study the soil profile pictured below. Identify the layer or layers where each of the following is found.

_____ live animals

_____ rock

_____ minerals

_____ live plants

_____ organic matter

_____ top layer

_____ middle layer

_____ lowest layer

_____ topsoil

_____ subsoil

_____ tree roots

_____ boulders

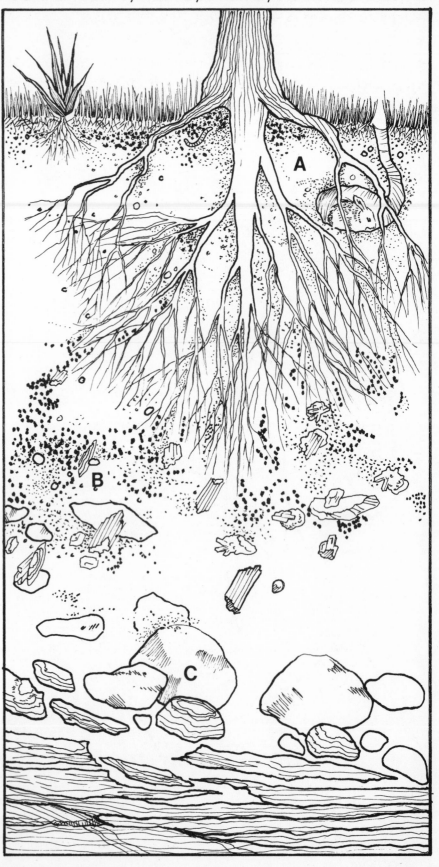

58

Making Crystals

People have always been fascinated by the incredible beauty of crystals. Crystals come in a wide variety of shapes.

Cut out each of the crystal patterns on the solid line. Then fold along the dotted lines. Tape the sides together. Match the common crystal shapes drawn here with the ones you have created.

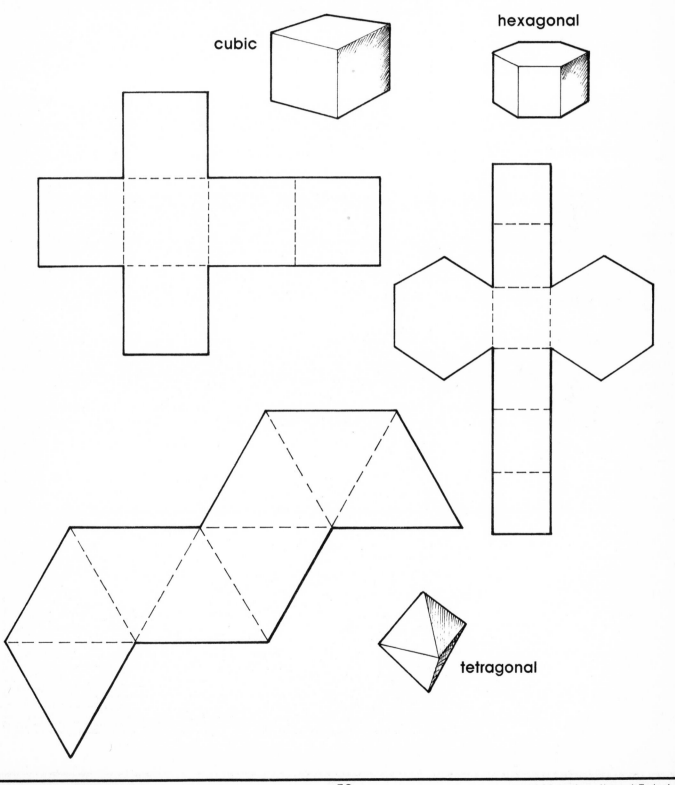

59

Mohs Hardness Scale

Name _____

One of the most useful properties used for identification of a mineral is its hardness. The Mohs hardness scale measures a mineral's hardness by means of a simple scratch test.

Name the mineral that belongs in each step of the Mohs Hardness Scale chart.

Mohs Hardness Scale		
Hardness	**Mineral**	**Common Tests**
1		Fingernail will scratch it.
2		
3		Fingernail will not scratch it; a copper penny will.
4		Knife blade or window glass will scratch it.
5		
6		Will scratch a steel knife or window glass.
7		
8		
9		
10		Will scratch all common materials.

WORD BANK

Talc	diamond	Gypsum	Corundum
Calcite	Topaz	Fluorite	Quartz
Apatite	Feldspar/Orthoclase		

Name That Mineral

Name _____

One can identify many minerals by carefully observing their physical characteristics. **Some** of these characteristics are:

Hardness — This is determined with a scratch test.

Color — Color depends on the substances that make up the crystals. Varies greatly.

Luster — This refers to how light reflects off the mineral.

Enough information has been given to you here to help you find the unknown minerals and fill in the chart.

Hardness Scale		
Hardness	Mineral	Common Tests
1	Talc	Fingernail will scratch it.
2	Gypsum/ Kaolinite	
3	Mica/ Calcite	A copper penny will scratch it.
4	Fluorite	Knife blade or window glass will scratch it.
5	Apatite/ Hornblende	
6	Feldspar	Will scratch a steel knife or window glass.
7	Quartz	
8	Topaz	
9	Corundum	
10	Diamond	Will scratch all common materials.

Color	Mineral
White:	Quartz, Feldspar, Calcite, Kaolinite, Talc
Yellow:	Quartz, Kaolinite
Black:	Hornblende, Mica
Gray:	Feldspar, Gypsum
Colorless:	Quartz, Calcite, Gypsum

Luster	Mineral
Glassy:	Quartz, Feldspar, Hornblende
Pearly:	Mica, Gypsum, Talc
Dull:	Kaolinite

THE UNKNOWN MINERALS —

Hardness	Color	Luster	Mineral
Will scratch a steel knife or window glass.	yellow	glassy	
Will scratch a steel knife or window glass.	gray	glassy	
A copper penny will scratch it.	black	pearly	
Fingernail will scratch it.	white	pearly	
Knife blade or window glass will scratch it.	black	glassy	

Classy Rocks

Name _____

There are three main groups of rock: **igneous** rock, **metamorphic** rock, and **sedimentary** rock. Each of the rocks pictured on this page belongs to one of these groups. Fill in the definitions. Then, in the space below each picture, tell which group each rock belongs to.

granite
_____

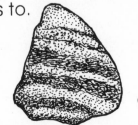
gneiss
_____

marble
_____

limestone
_____

shale
_____

basalt
_____

sandstone
_____

slate
_____

obsidian
_____

conglomerate
_____

Kind of Rock	Definition
Igneous	
Sedimentary	
Metamorphic	

DEFINITIONS

layers of loose material which solidified

cooled magma

rock that has been changed into a new rock

Rocks and Minerals

Name _____

Use what you have learned about rocks and minerals to complete this puzzle.

Across

2. An uneven break
3. Substance with 3-dimensional plane faces
4. Feel of a surface when rubbed
6. Measured with Mohs Scale
8. Quartz is an example of a _____ .

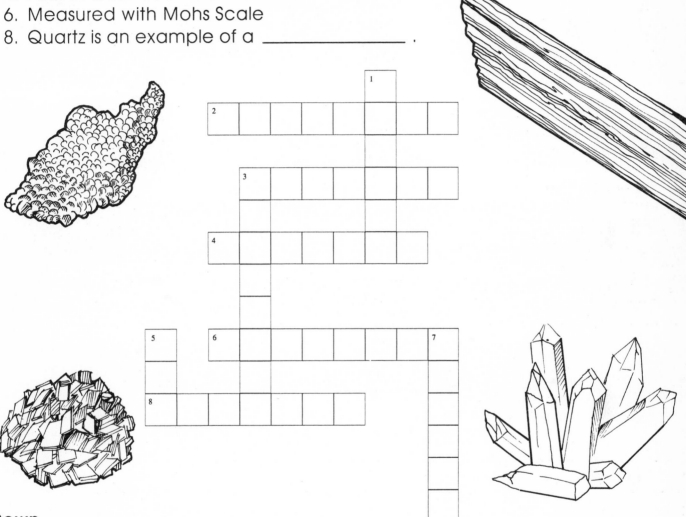

Down

1. Light reflected from a mineral's surface
3. Smooth break in a mineral
5. Large mineral crystal with brilliant color
7. A _____ test shows the color of a mineral when it is rubbed into a fine powder.

WORD BANK

hardness	crystal	streak
gem	cleavage	texture
fracture	luster	mineral

Whose Fault Is It?

A crack in the Earth's bedrock is called a fault. There are two types of faults, the <u>strike-slip fault</u> and the <u>dip-slip fault.</u>
California is known for the San Andreas Fault. Draw the San Andreas Fault on the map of California, then label the two different kinds of faults.

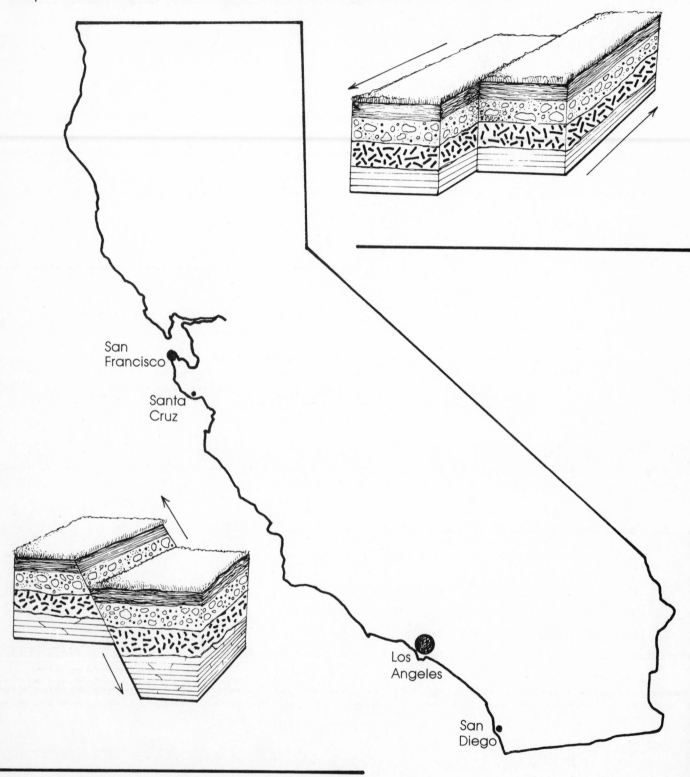

Drifting Continents

About 250 million years ago there was one continent called Pangaea (Figure **A**).
By 45 million years ago the land mass split into seven land masses (Figure **B**).
Label the land masses in Figure **B**.

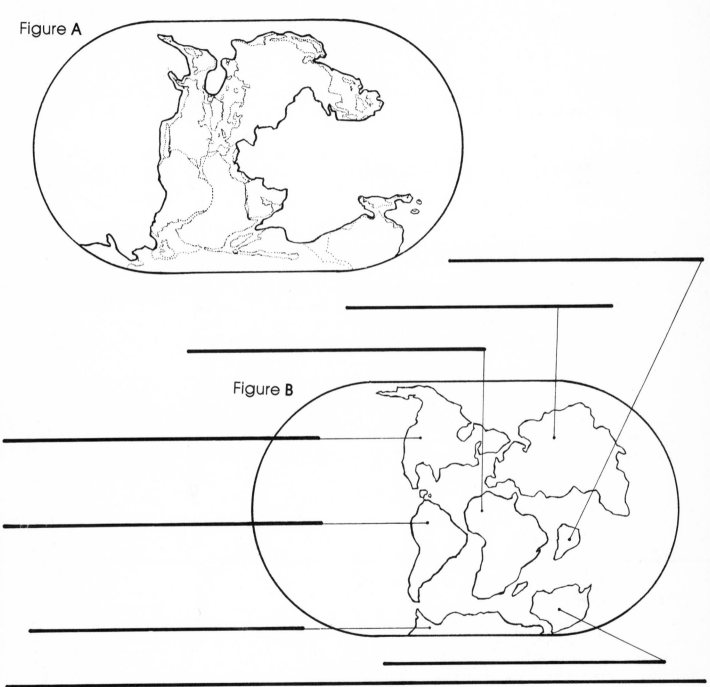

Figure **A**

Figure **B**

WORD BANK

North America   South America   Eurasia
Africa   India   Australia
Antarctica

"Broken Plates"

Name_____

Below are puzzle pieces of the Earth's seven major plates. Cut out the plates and glue them on a separate sheet of paper. Label the plates.

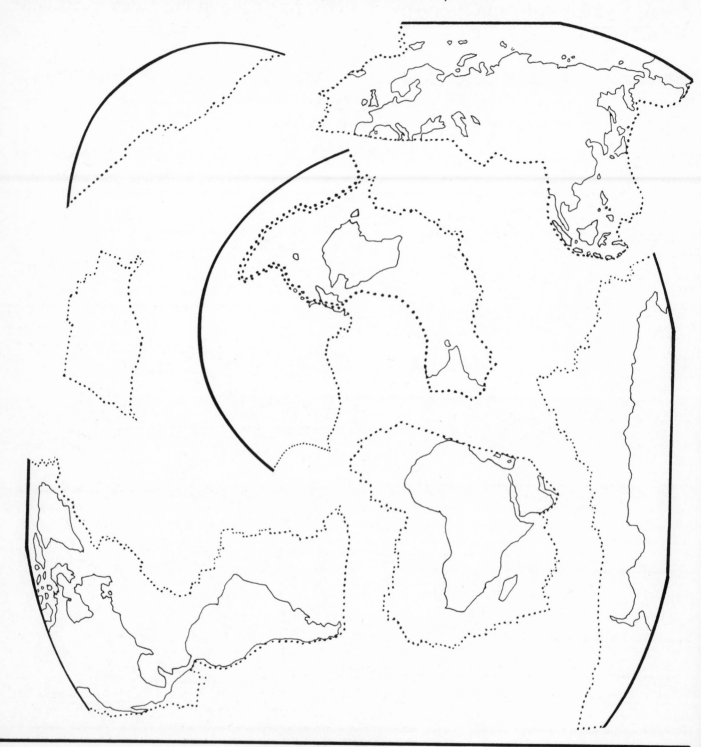

WORD BANK

Antarctic Plate

Pacific Plate   American Plate   Eurasian Plate

African Plate   Nazca Plate   Indo-Australian Plate

Earth's Moving Plates

Name _____

The Earth's crust is made of rigid plates that are always moving. The boundaries of some of these plates are along the edges of the continents, while others are in the middle of the ocean. The map on this page shows the major plates near North and South America.

Using an encyclopedia or some other source, label the eight plates pictured below.

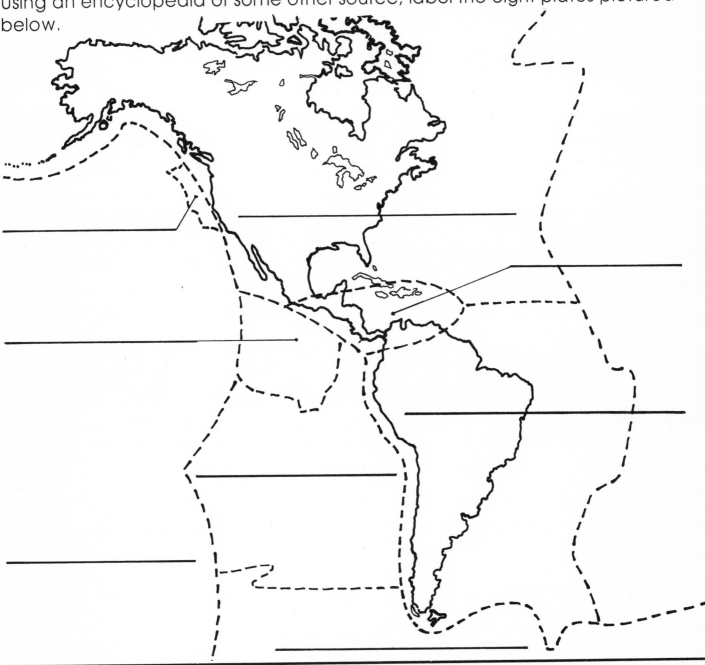

WORD BANK

Gorda Plate   North American Plate   Cocos Plate
Pacific Plate   South American Plate   Nazca Plate
Antarctic Plate   Caribbean Plate

Bending the Earth's Crust

Name _____

According to the theory of plate tectonics, the earth's crust is broken into about twenty **plates.** These plates are slowly moving. The edges of some of these plates are moving toward each other. A **trench** is formed when one plate bends and dives under another. The diving edge then descends into the earth's hot, **mantle** and starts melting into **magma**. The magma can then rise and break through the earth's crust and burst out of a **volcano**. The edge of the above-riding plate crumples, resulting in a mountain range.

Label the diagram below.

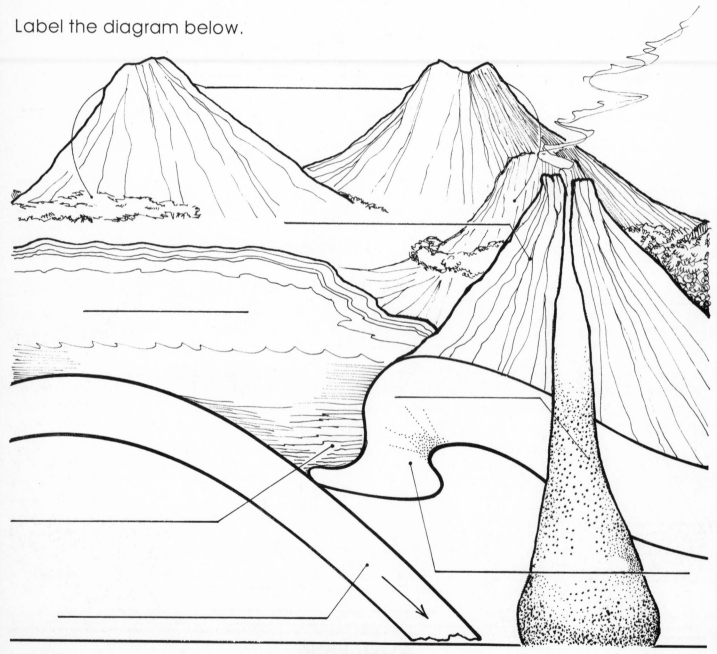

WORD BANK

	ocean	trench	magma
volcano	continent	descending plate	above-riding plate

Volcanoes

Name_____

Label the parts of this volcano using the words from the **WORD BANK**.

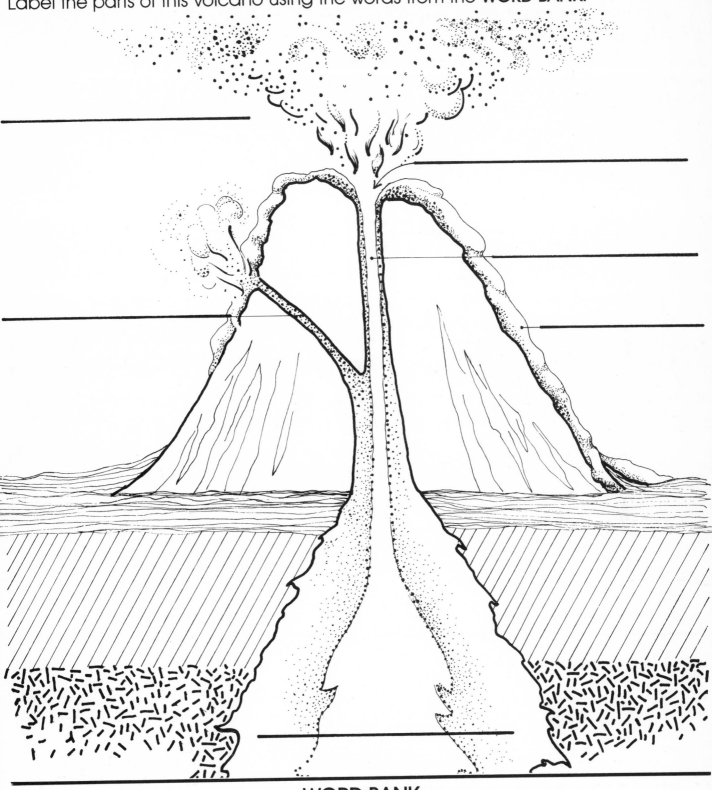

WORD BANK

central vent   lava   conduit

magma chamber   side vent   gas and dust

"Ring of Fire"

Name_____

There are more than 500 active volcanoes in the world. More than half of these encircle the Pacific Ocean in an area called the "Ring of Fire." Color the region known as the "Ring of Fire." Research this region, locate and label some of its well-known volcanoes.

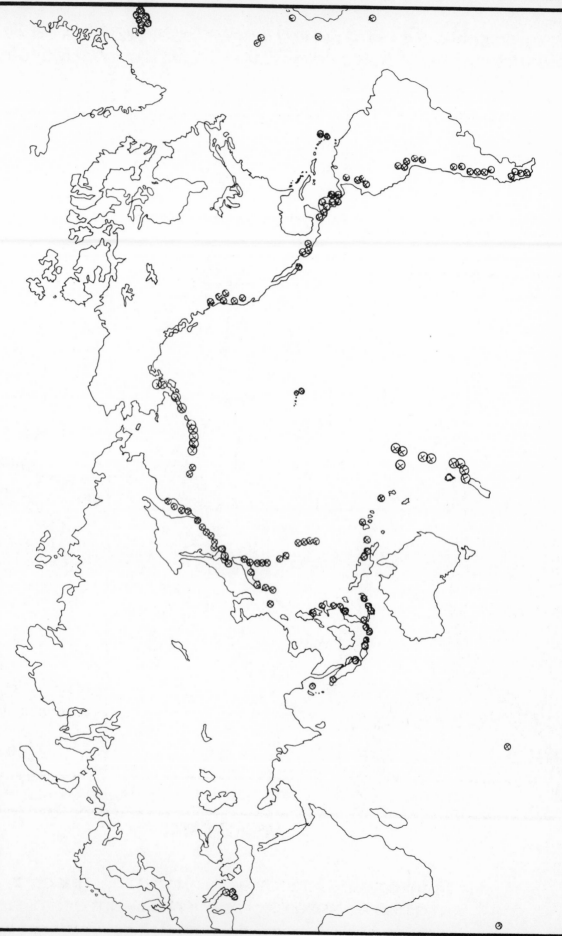

© 1991 Instructional Fair, Inc.

Volcanic Cones

Name_____

Volcanic cones can be classified by their shapes. Label the three different kinds of volcanic cones pictured below. Label the parts of the volcanoes.

_____ Cone   _____ Cone   _____ Cone

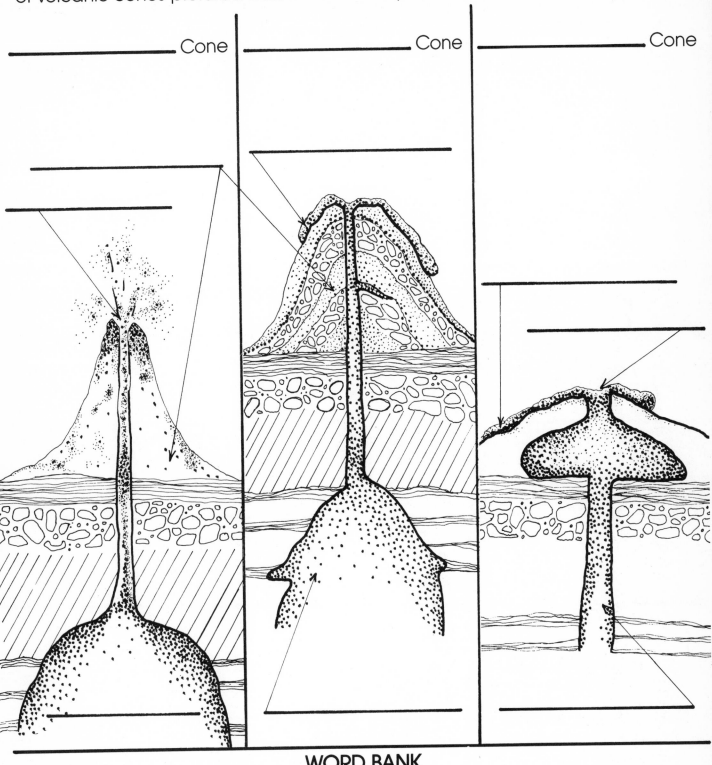

WORD BANK

Shield   Composite   Cinder   magma
vent   lava flow   cinders

Forming Igneous Rock

Name _____

Igneous rock is one of the three major types of rock. It is formed by the hardening of molten rock (magma). Magma does not always reach the earth's surface as lava erupting from a volcano. It often forms other igneous rock structures underground.

Label the igneous rock structures shown here.

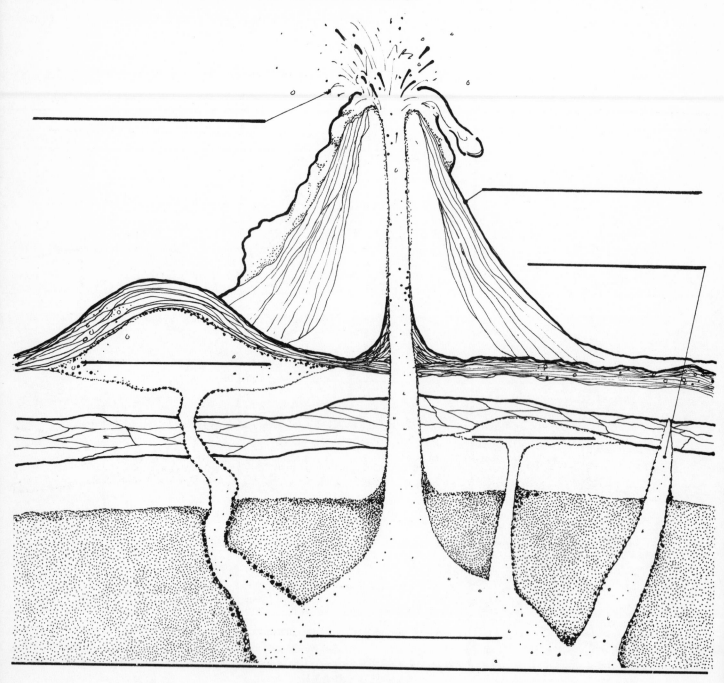

WORD BANK

laccolith   sill   dike   batholith
lava   volcano

Drilling for Oil

Name _____

Most oil is found thousands of feet beneath the surface of the earth. It is trapped beneath layers of nonporous rock, such as shale, which will not allow the oil to pass through. Often pockets of natural gas will also form where there is oil. Oil companies drill for oil using large drills that grind through the ground and rock.

The illustration below shows one example of where oil can be found. Label the illustration.

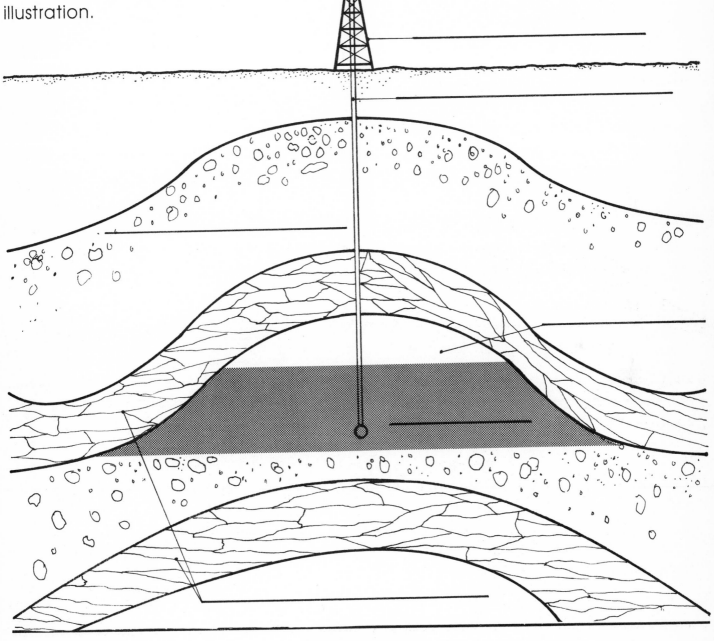

WORD BANK

oil   nonporous rock   natural gas
derrick   drill pipe   porous rock

Coral Reefs

Name_____

Three types of coral reefs are pictured below.
1. Label each type of coral reef.
2. Label the features that are enclosed by the reef.
3. Number the steps in the formation of an atoll.

_____

_____

Step No. _____

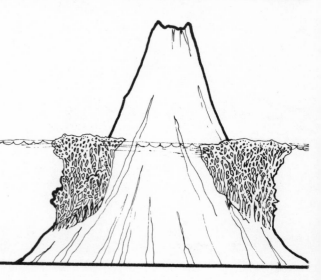

_____

_____

Step No. _____

_____

_____

Step No. _____

WORD BANK

fringing reef	barrier reef	atoll
inactive volcano	island	lagoon

Groundwater at Work

Name _____

Groundwater is water in the ground that is near the surface. People remove groundwater with wells. Label the pictures below with the terms found in the **Word Bank**.

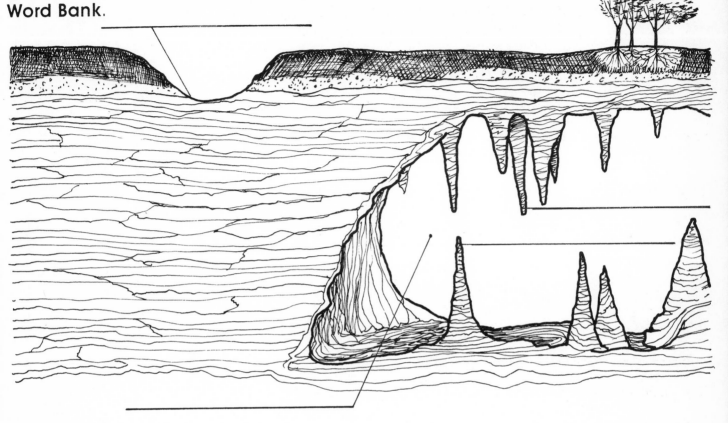

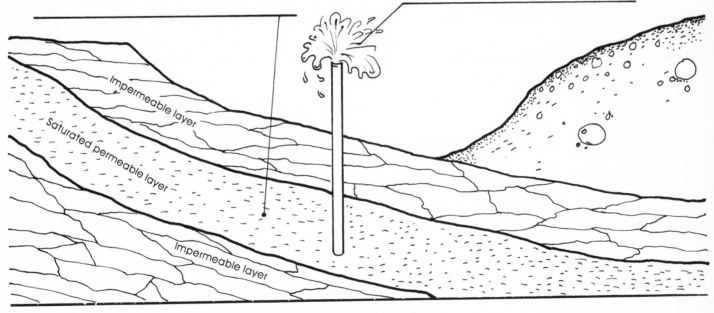

Impermeable layer

Saturated permeable layer

Impermeable layer

WORD BANK

sinkhole	stalactite	stalagmite	cave
artesian well	aquifer		

The Ocean Floor

Name_____

Label the features of the ocean floor.

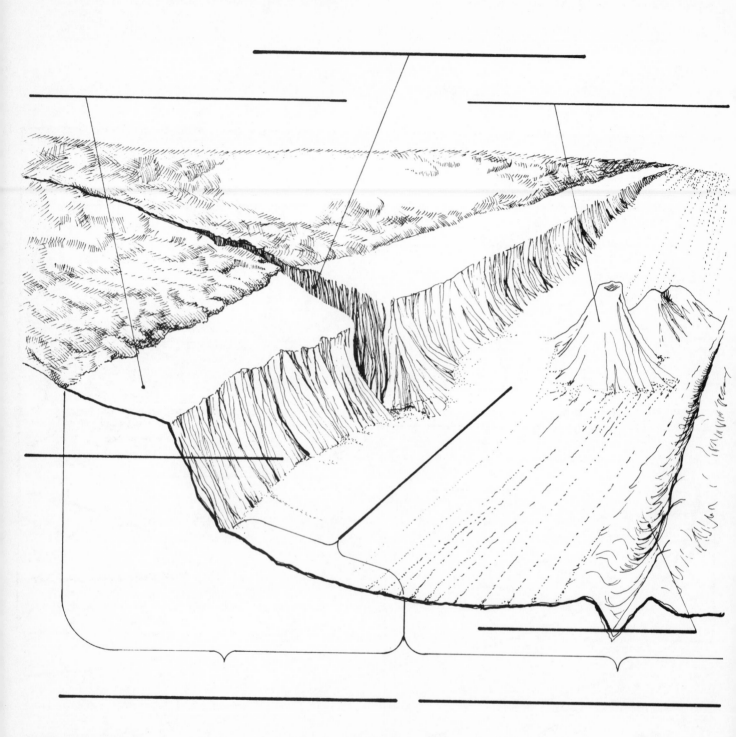

WORD BANK

continental shelf   trench   continental slope
submarine canyon   mountain   continental rise
ocean basin   continental margin

Ocean Currents

Name _____

Water moves within the oceans in streams called currents. Label the ocean currents pictured on the map.

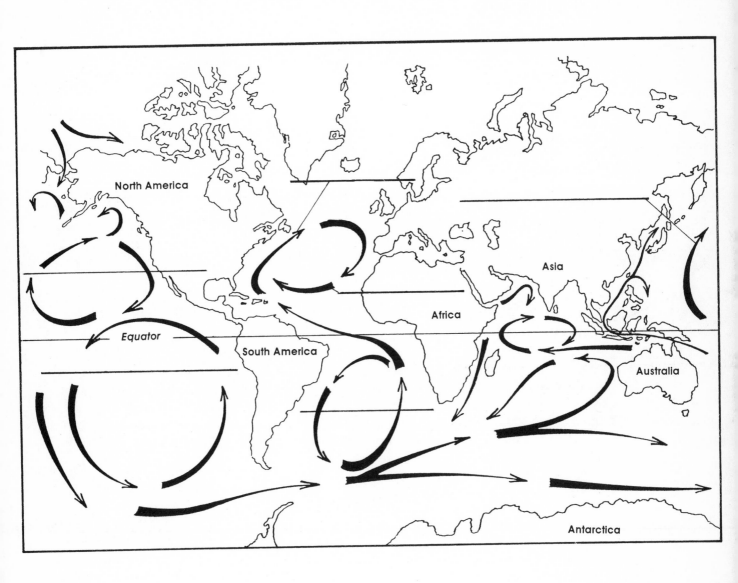

WORD BANK

California Current   Peru Current   Gulf Stream
Japan Current   Canary Current   Brazil Current

Landform Regions of the United States

Name _____

The continental United States can be divided into several major landform regions. Label each region using the list found in the **Word Bank**.

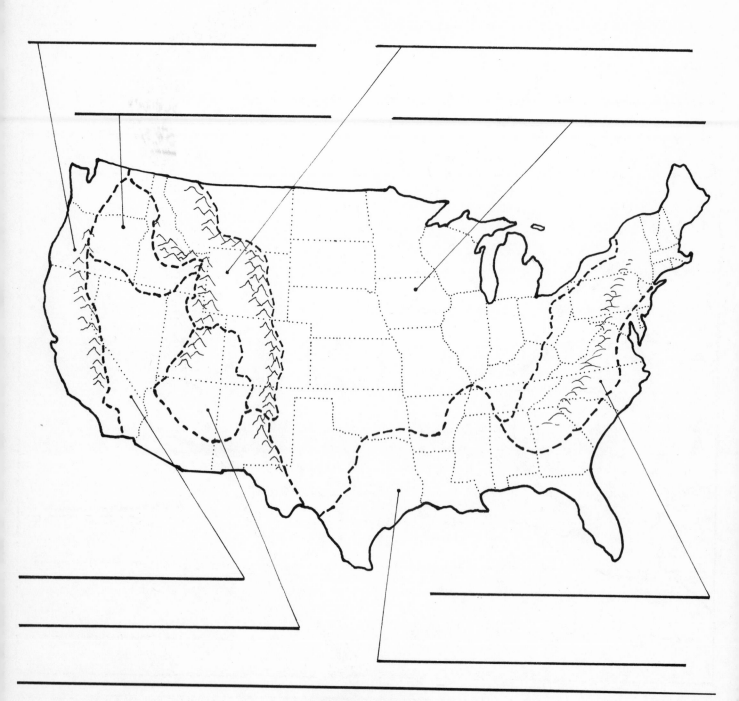

WORD BANK

Interior Plains   Columbia Plateau   Rocky Mountains
Great Basin   Colorado Plateau   Coastal Lowlands
Pacific Ranges and Lowlands   Appalachian Highlands

Topographic Maps

A topographic map uses contour lines to show the elevation and slope of hills, valleys, and other natural features. Label the various land features and elements of the topographic map pictured below.

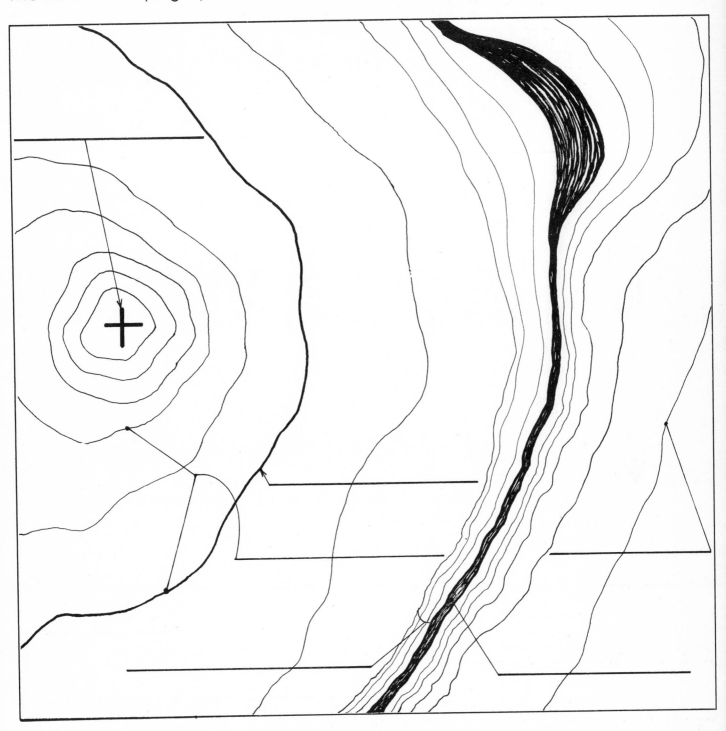

WORD BANK

contour line	index contour line	mountain top
steep slope	gentle slope	river

Benchmark to Benchmark

Name_____

Use the benchmarks on the map below to help you draw the contour lines. The contour lines should be drawn at 20 foot intervals.

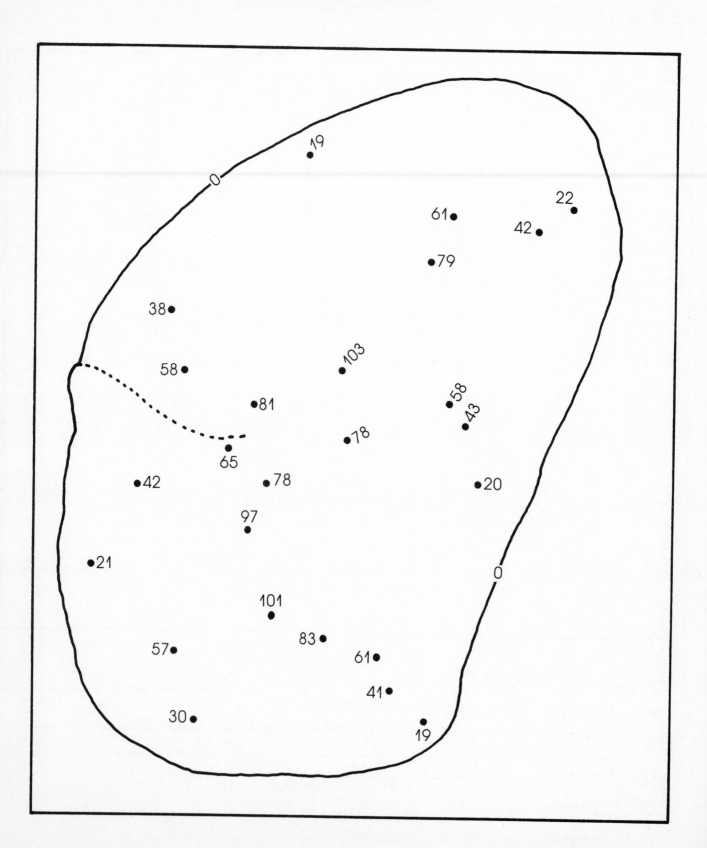

Topographical Maps

Topographical maps give the geographical positions and elevations of both manmade and natural features. Using the contour lines and contour intervals, label the elevations of the features on this map.

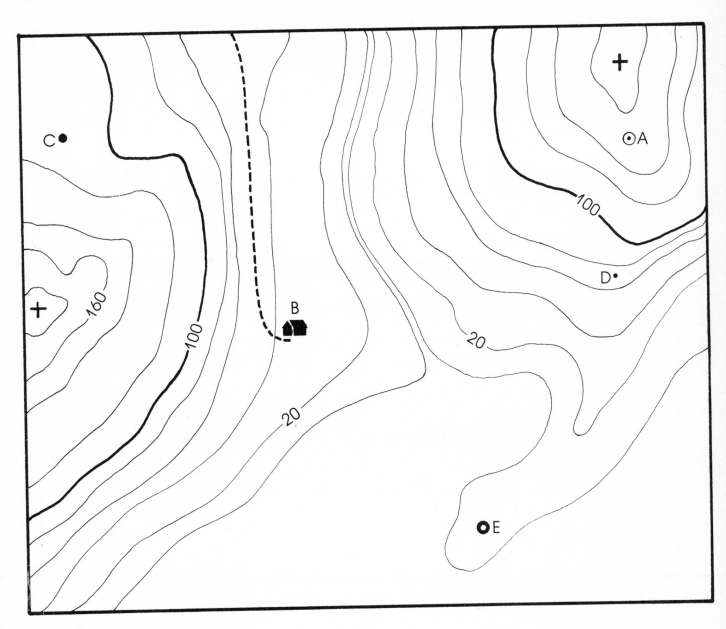

FEATURE   ELEVATION

A   between _____ and _____ feet

B   between _____ and _____ feet

C   between _____ and _____ feet

D   between _____ and _____ feet

E   between _____ and _____ feet

Meandering River

Name_____

A river goes through different stages of development as it erodes its channel.
Label the parts of the river.

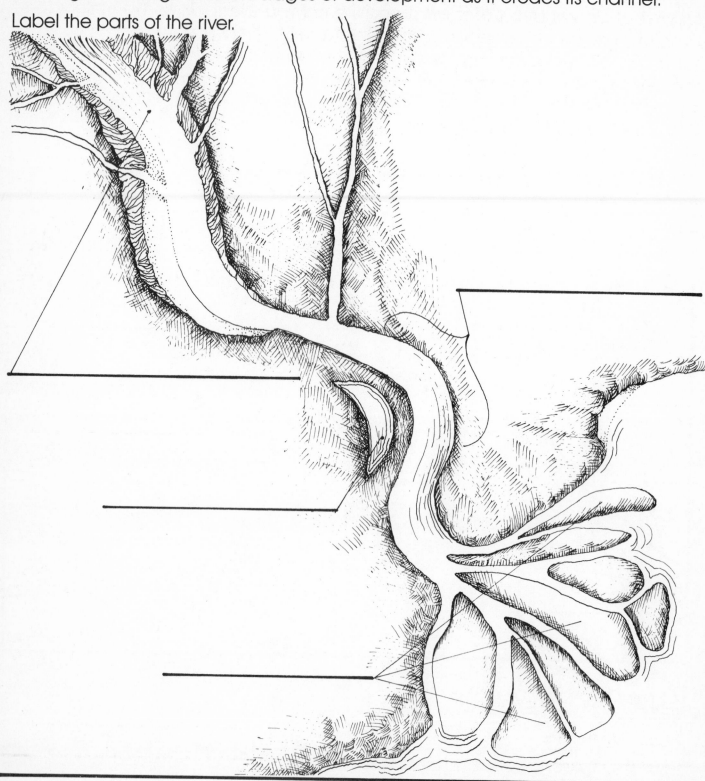

WORD BANK

young river   oxbow lake   meander   delta

River System

A river may begin its journey to the sea high up in the mountains as a melting glacier, or as a number of small streams and brooks high up in the hills. As the river flows downhill the moving water reshapes the land by carrying away sand, stones, and clay. The river and all the water that flows into it make up the **river system**.

Label the parts of the river system.

WORD BANK

glacier	lake	waterfall	rapids
delta	meander	alluvial fan	tributary
oxbow lake			

83

Glaciers

Tons of ice and trapped rock scrape and grind mountain walls as a glacier creeps down a mountain. The tremendous force of the moving glacier re-shapes the mountain slopes in its path, leaving behind deposits of rock.

Label the formations made by the moving glacier.

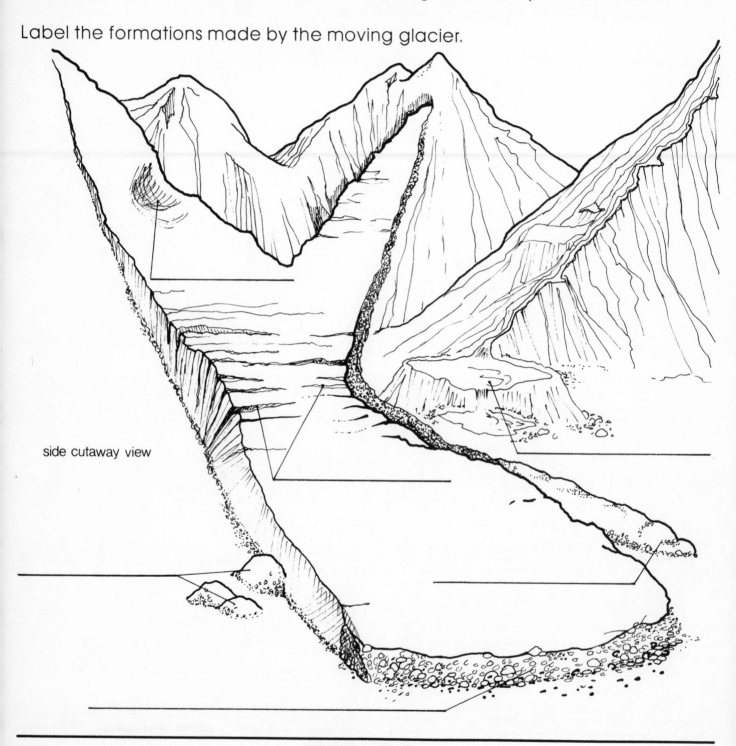

side cutaway view

WORD BANK

esker	drumlin	kettle lake
terminal moraine	crevasses	cirque

84

You're All Wet!!!

Name_____

It's a wet day. The symbols on the weather map show eight different forms of precipitation occuring around the country. Label each form of precipitation.

WORD BANK

drizzle	rain	sleet	snow
shower	fog	hail	thunderstorm

Gentle Breezes

On the chart below list the wind speed and wind direction for the cities that are listed.

City	Wind Direction	Wind Speed
Los Angeles		
San Francisco		
Seattle		
Denver		
Chicago		
Toronto		
Miami		

Symbol	Wind Speed Km/h
◎	calm
—	0-4
⌐	5-13
⌐	14-22
⌐	23-32
⌐	33-41
⌐	42-50
⌐	51-49
⌐	60-69
⌐	70-78
⌐	79-87
◢	88-96

Weather Map Symbols

Name _____

Weather maps, like the one on this page, provide data from which meteorologists prepare weather forecasts. To accurately read a weather map you must be able to understand the weather map symbols.

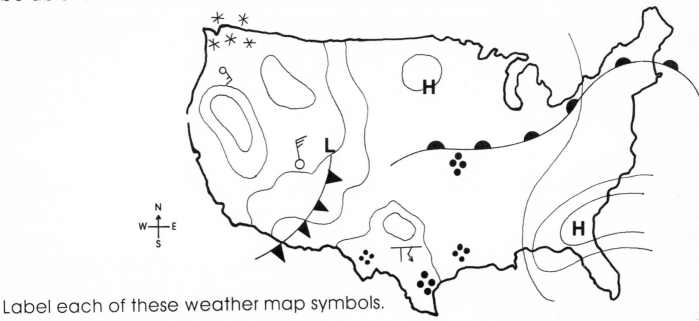

Label each of these weather map symbols.

WORD BANK

rain	clear skies	thunderstorm	cloudy
snow	partly cloudy	cold front	occluded front
high pressure	warm front	stationary front	low pressure
wind speed and direction			

Using a Weather Map

Name _____

Weather maps show the recorded weather conditions over a large geographic area. Use the map shown on this page along with what you have learned about weather symbols to complete the chart.

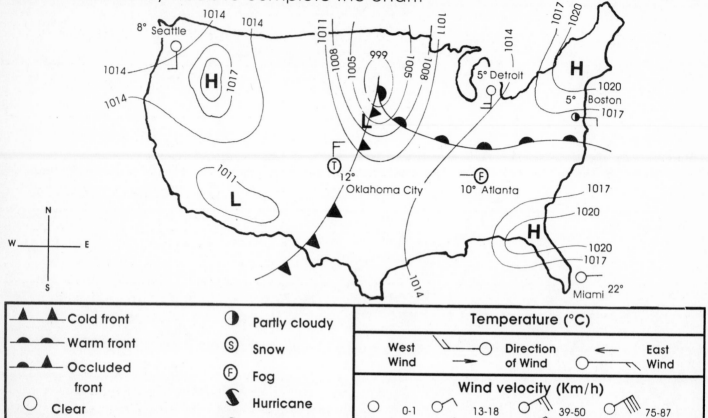

City	Temp.	Cloud Cover/ Weather Condition	Wind Velocity	Wind Direction
Seattle				
Atlanta				
Detroit				
Miami				
Oklahoma City				
Boston				

Precipitation

Name _____

Precipitation is water vapor that condenses and falls to the earth. Depending on the conditions in the atmosphere, precipitation can fall in a number of forms. The symbol for each form is pictured below.

Identify each form of precipitation by drawing its symbol next to its description.

Symbols

rain

drizzle

rain showers

sleet

snow

hail

fog

Symbol	Definition
	Clouds that form close to the ground.
	Droplets that freeze as they get closer to the ground.
	Light mist of droplets falling to the earth.
	Droplets of water freeze around ice crystals as they bounce up and down within a storm cloud. Fall to earth when they get heavy.
	Vapor that changes directly into crystalline flakes because of freezing temperatures.
	Water vapor that forms droplets and falls to the earth.
	Large amount of droplets falling to the earth.

Use another source to help you complete this chart.

Weather	Symbol	Definition
thunderstorm		
lightning		
squall		

Moving Weather Systems

Name _____

A careful study of the daily weather maps found in your newspaper will show that weather systems are constantly on the move.

You will need four copies of this page. Use a new sheet every day for three days to copy that day's weather pattern (frontal systems, pressure cells, precipitation) from your newspaper. Study the movement of the pattern. Then draw a weather pattern predicting where the weather systems will move on the next day.

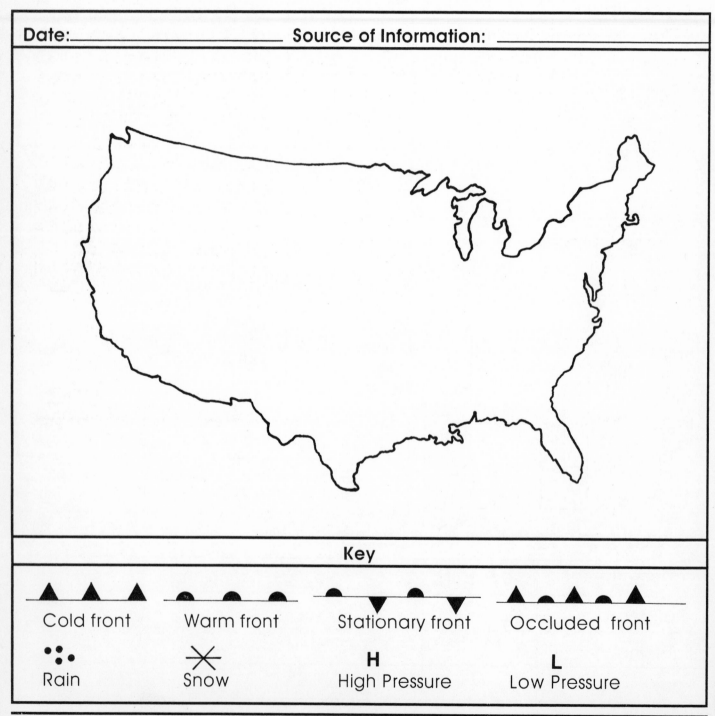

Date:_____ **Source of Information:** _____

Key

Cold front	Warm front	Stationary front	Occluded front

Rain   Snow   **H** High Pressure   **L** Low Pressure

Relative Humidity

Name_____

Relative humidity is the amount of water vapor that the air can hold at a certain temperature. Relative humidity is measured with a hygrometer.
Use the table to find the relative humidity for the data recorded on the chart below.

Day	Dry Temp.	Wet Temp.	Relative Humidity
Mon.	22°	21°	
Tue.	23°	21°	
Wed.	21°	19°	
Thur.	19°	18°	
Fri.	18°	15°	
Sat.	19°	15°	
Sun.	17°	13°	

Dry bulb temp. °C	Difference between wet and dry temperatures							
	1°	2°	3°	4°	5°	6°	7°	8°
15°	90	80	71	61	53	44	36	27
16°	90	81	71	63	54	46	38	30
17°	90	81	72	64	55	47	40	32
18°	91	82	73	65	57	49	41	34
19°	91	82	74	65	58	50	43	36
20°	91	83	74	66	59	51	44	37
21°	91	83	75	67	60	53	46	39
22°	92	83	76	68	61	54	47	40
23°	92	84	76	69	62	55	48	42
24°	92	84	77	69	62	56	49	43
25°	92	84	77	70	63	57	50	44
26°	92	85	78	71	64	58	51	46
27°	92	85	78	71	65	58	52	47

Use your data to make a graph of the relative humidity.

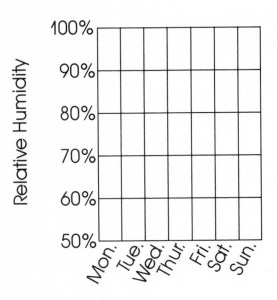

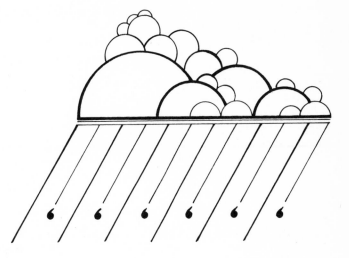

Air Currents

Name _____

Name the three air current phenomena pictured below using words from the Word Bank. Then fill in each explanation.

This picture shows: _____

    Explanation: _____

_____

_____

_____

_____

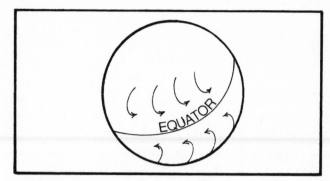

This picture shows: _____

    Explanation: _____

_____

_____

_____

_____

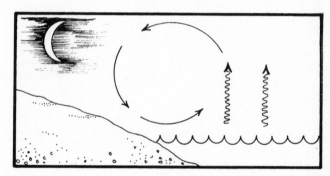

This picture shows: _____

    Explanation: _____

_____

_____

_____

_____

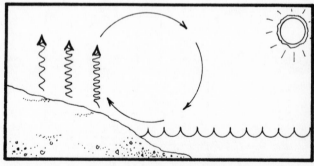

WORD BANK

a land breeze
a sea breeze
the Coriolis effect

EXPLANATIONS

The earth's rotation affects the paths of winds.

During day, cooler air from sea replaces warm air over shore.

At night, cool air over shore replaces warm air over sea.

The Water Cycle

Name _____

The never-ending circulation of the waters of the earth from the oceans, to the air, and to the land is called the water cycle. Label the three major steps in the water cycle. Then explain how the water cycle works in your own words.

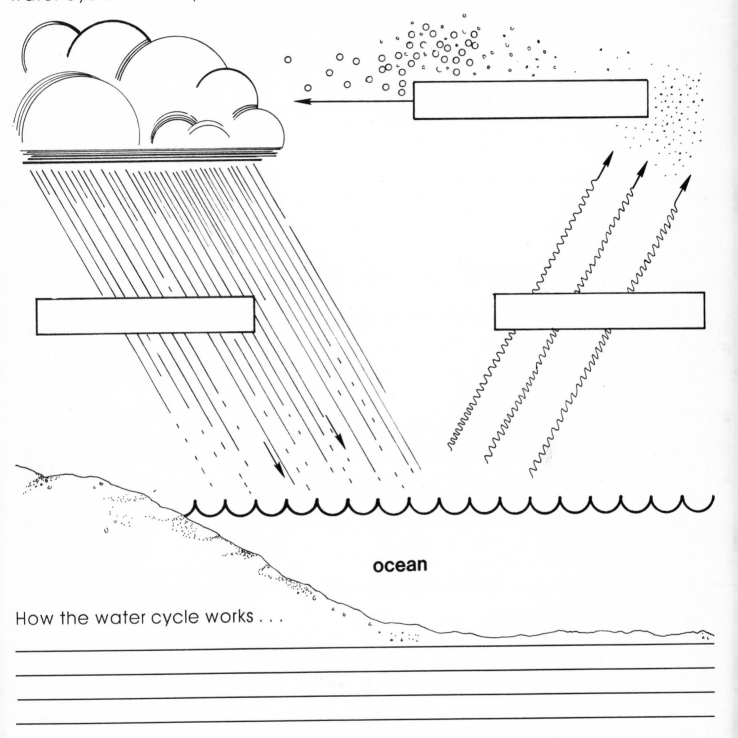

ocean

How the water cycle works . . .

_____

_____

_____

_____

_____

_____

WORD BANK

condensation   precipitation   evaporation

What's Up Front?

A front is where two air masses meet. Changes in the weather take place along a front.

Label the two fronts and the kinds of air masses in the illustrations below.

_____ front

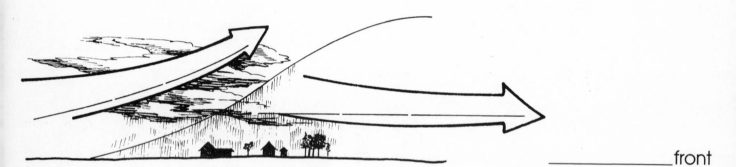

_____ front

Label the four kinds of fronts that are represented by the symbols below.

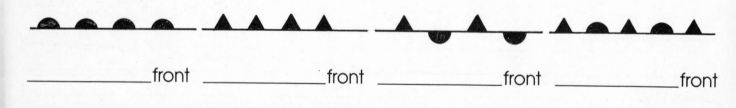

_____ front _____ front _____ front _____ front

WORD BANK

warm air mass   cold air mass   cold front
warm front   stationary front   occluded front

A Cold Front

The illustration below is a front between two air masses. The cooler air mass is replacing the warmer air mass.

Label the cloud types associated with the cold front pictured below.

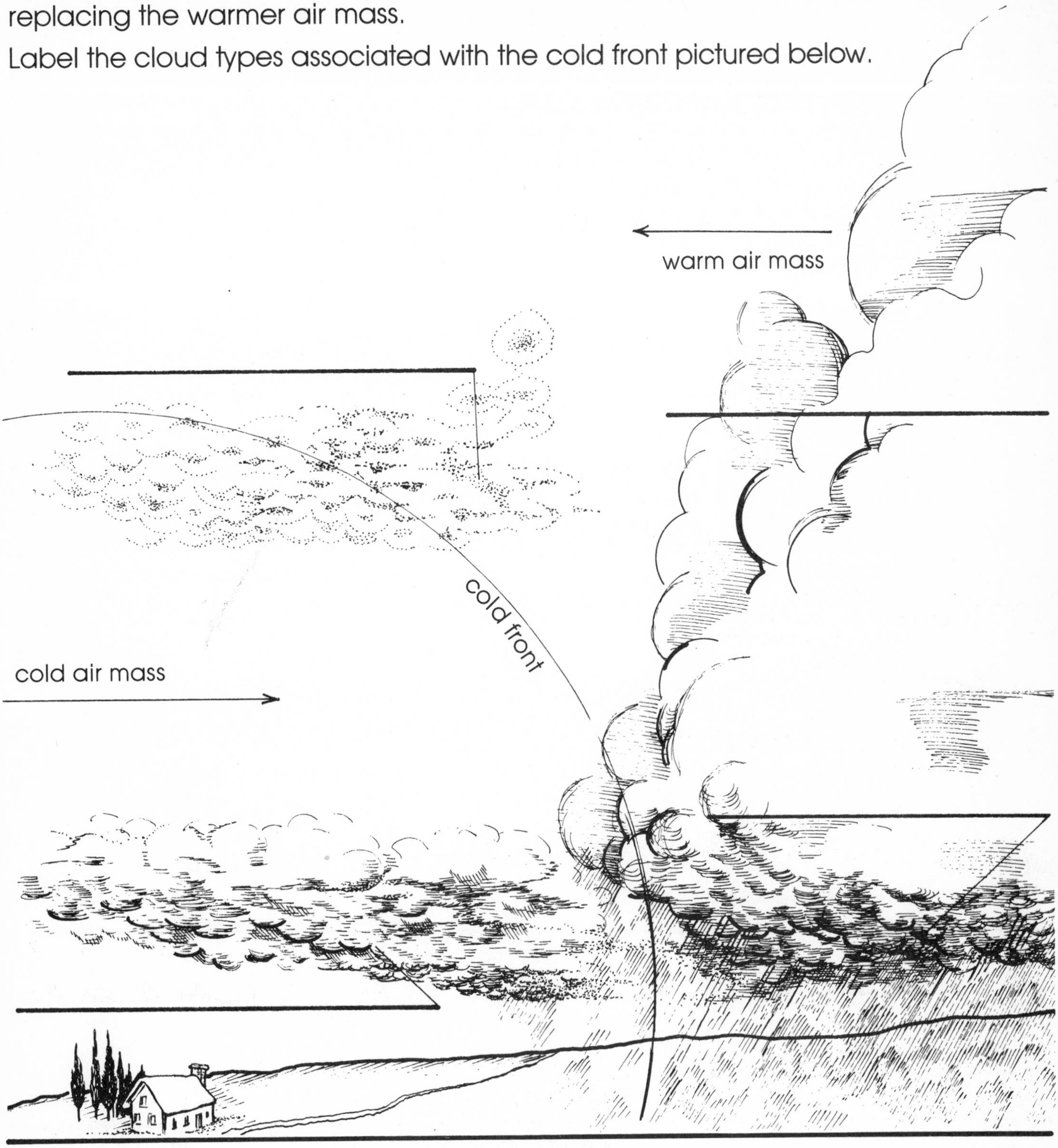

warm air mass

cold front

cold air mass

WORD BANK

cumulonimbus   altocumulus   nimbostratus   stratocumulus

A Warm Front

The illustration below is a front between two air masses. A warm air mass is pushing a cold air mass.

Label the cloud types associated with the warm front pictured below.

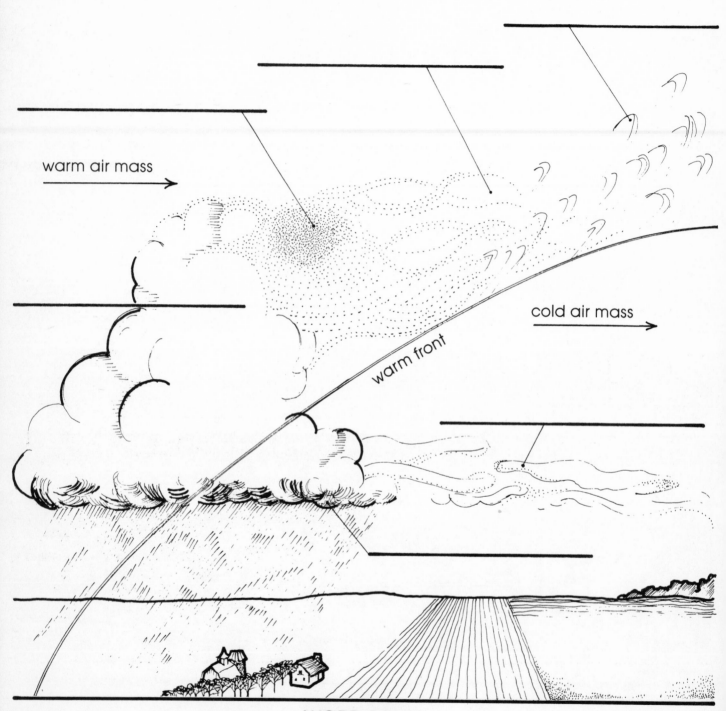

warm air mass

cold air mass

warm front

WORD BANK

cumulus   altostratus   cirrostratus
cirrus   stratus   nimbostratus

Cloud Types

Label the cloud types pictured below.

WORD BANK

stratus   cumulus   cirrus
altostratus   altocumulus   cirrocumulus
cirrostratus   cumulonimbus   nimbostratus
stratocumulus

Earth Science IF8755   97   © 1991 Instructional Fair, Inc.

Clouds and Weather

Name _____

Different types of clouds are often associated with a specific kind of weather. Four different kinds of clouds are pictured below. Write the name of the cloud type, a description of the cloud, and the kind of weather associated with each one.

Cloud Type	Name	Description	Associated Weather

WORD BANK

thunderstorms	cumulonimbus	cumulus
fair, sometimes showers	thin, wispy clouds	stratus
steady drizzle	tall, dark and billowing	fair
smooth sheets, or layers	piles of "puffy" clouds	cirrus

Tomorrow's Weather Forecast

Name _____

Check the accuracy of the weather forecasts in your area for the next week. Complete the chart by writing the forecast for "tomorrow's" weather and then recording the actual weather for that day. Indicate whether or not the forecast was accurate by circling yes or no.

	Date	Temp. Range	Precipi-tation	Wind Speed	Wind Direction	Sky Condition	Accurate Forecast? (Circle.)
Forecast							Yes
Actual							No
Forecast							Yes
Actual							No
Forecast							Yes
Actual							No
Forecast							Yes
Actual							No
Forecast							Yes
Actual							No
Forecast							Yes
Actual							No
Forecast							Yes
Actual							No

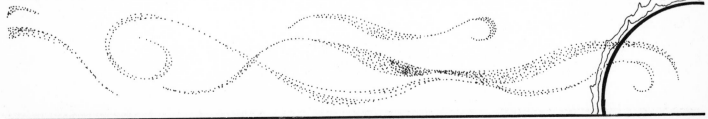

Weather Tools

Name_____

Meteorologists use many instruments to gather their data.
Label each of these weather instruments.

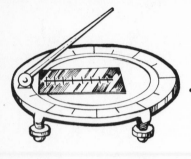

_____

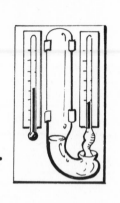

_____

_____

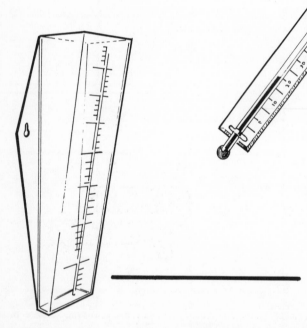

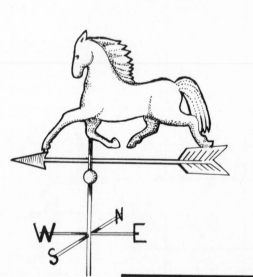

_____

_____

_____

___

WORD BANK

nephoscope   thermometer   barometer
hygrometer   rain gauge   vane
            anemometer

Weather Instruments

Name _____

Meteorologists use a variety of instruments to gather data. Many of these instruments are pictured below. Identify each instrument and tell what it measures.

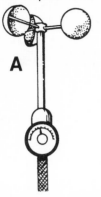

A

B

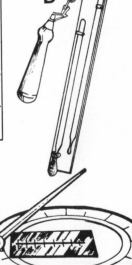

C

D

	Weather Instrument	It Measures . . .
A		
B		
C		
D		
E		
F		
G		

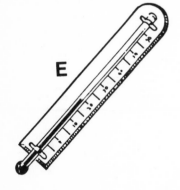

E

F

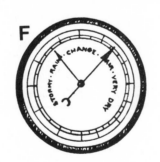

G

WORD BANK

temperature
anemometer
weathervane
rain gauge
wind direction

relative humidity
thermometer
hygrometer
precipitation
cloud altitude and direction

atmospheric (air) pressure
barometer
nephoscope
wind speed

Puzzling Weather

Name _____

Sometimes even the weatherperson is puzzled by the weather, but don't let these weather terms puzzle you.

Across

3. Place where two air masses meet
5. Twisting funnel cloud
6. Rain that freezes as it falls
8. Scale used to measure wind speed
11. Measures air pressure
12. Measures wind direction and speed
13. Sound made by rapidly heating and expanding air caused by lightning
14. Layer clouds

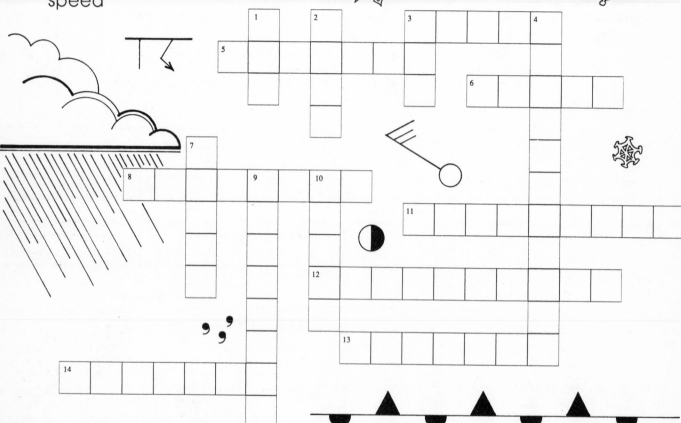

Down

1. Cloudy weather occurs in _____ -pressure areas.
2. Soft, white crystalline flakes
3. A thick, ground-level mist
4. Measures temperature
7. Precipitation is measured with a rain _____ .
9. Prediction of weather in the future
10. Calculates distance of clouds by echoing radio waves

WORD BANK

barometer	sleet	thermometer	stratus	fog
front	thunder	forecast	snow	Beaufort
anemometer	low	radar	tornado	gauge

Answer Key

A Scientist's Equipment

Name_____

Scientists use many different kinds of special equipment in a laboratory. Label the equipment below.

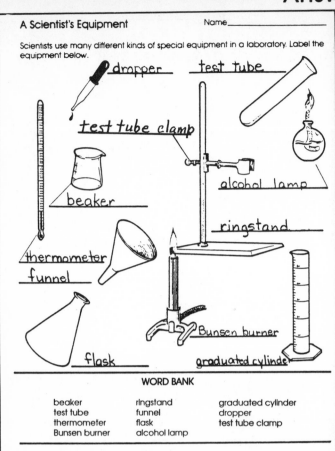

dropper
test tube
test tube clamp
alcohol lamp
beaker
ringstand
thermometer
funnel
Bunsen burner
flask
graduated cylinder

WORD BANK

beaker	ringstand	graduated cylinder
test tube	funnel	dropper
thermometer	flask	test tube clamp
Bunsen burner	alcohol lamp	

Page 1

How Long Is It?

Name_____

The meter is the standard unit of measurement when measuring the length of an object or the distance between two objects. Use either <u>kilometer</u>, <u>meter</u>, <u>centimeter</u> or <u>millimeter</u> to label the unit that would be used to measure the objects in the pictures below.

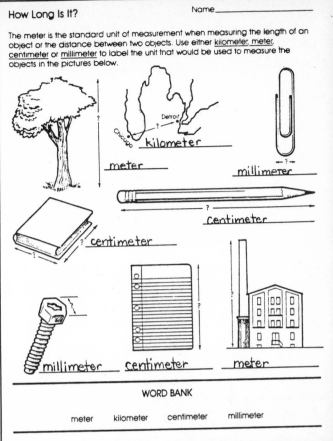

kilometer
meter
millimeter
centimeter
centimeter
millimeter
centimeter
meter

WORD BANK

meter   kilometer   centimeter   millimeter

Page 2

The Long and Short of It

Name_____

Weight, length, area and volume are properties of matter that scientists can measure. Scientists use the units of grams, meters and liters to measure these properties.

Write the abbreviation for each of these units of measurement.

Unit of Measure .	Abbreviation
gram	g
kilogram	kg
milligram	mg
meter	m
kilometer	km
centimeter	cm
millimeter	mm
square centimeters	cm^2
cubic centimeters	cm^3
liter	l
milliliter	ml

WORD BANK

g   kg   mg   m   km   cm
mm   cm²   cm³   l   ml

Page 3

Celsius vs. Fahrenheit

Name_____

The thermometer on this page compares the Celsius and Fahrenheit scales. Label the temperatures on the Celsius and Fahrenheit scales using the temperatures from the WORD BANK.

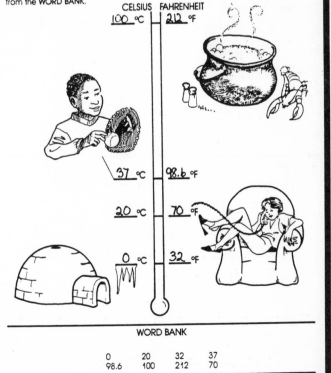

CELSIUS   FAHRENHEIT
100 °C   212 °F
37 °C   98.6 °F
20 °C   70 °F
0 °C   32 °F

WORD BANK

0   20   32   37
98.6   100   212   70

Page 4

Answer Key

Balances

Name _____

The mass of an object can be measured using a balance. Two common types of balances are the triple beam balance and the double pan balance.

Name each balance pictured below and then label the parts. The words in the Word Bank may be used more than once.

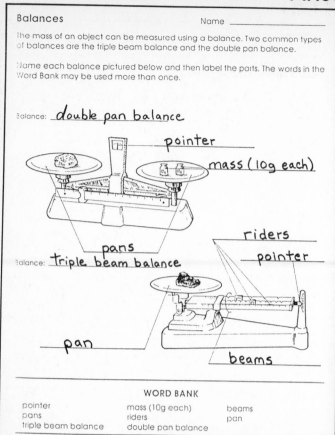

Balance: _double pan balance_

pointer

mass (10g each)

pans

Balance: _triple beam balance_

riders

pointer

pan

beams

WORD BANK

pointer	mass (10g each)	beams
pans	riders	pan
triple beam balance	double pan balance	

Page 5

Reading a Double Pan Balance

Name _____

To determine the weight of an object using a double pan balance, find the sum of masses needed to balance the two pans. Do this by making the pointer on the balance line up with the indicated line.

Find the mass of each of the objects pictured below.

Masses

5g 10g 20g 50g

1g

1. __59__ g

2. __37__ g

3. __88__ g

4. __46__ g

Page 6

Reading a Triple Beam Balance

Name _____

To determine the mass or weight of an object using a triple beam balance, find the sum of the masses shown on all the riders.

Find the mass indicated on each of the triple beam balances pictured below.

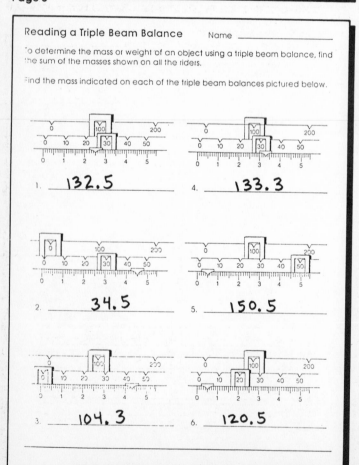

1. __132.5__

2. __34.5__

3. __104.3__

4. __133.3__

5. __150.5__

6. __120.5__

Page 7

Reading a Graduated Cylinder

Name _____

Small quantities of a liquid can be measured using a graduated cylinder. You may notice how the liquid curves up the side of the cylinder. To get an accurate reading, read the measurement at the bottom of the curve, or *meniscus*.

Read the following volumes.

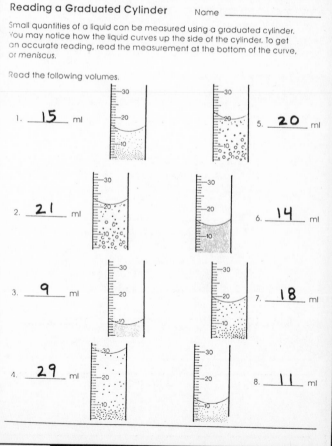

1. __15__ ml

2. __21__ ml

3. __9__ ml

4. __29__ ml

5. __20__ ml

6. __14__ ml

7. __18__ ml

8. __11__ ml

Page 8

Answer Key

Chemical Symbols

Name_____

Use the symbols to find the names of the elements needed to complete the puzzle.

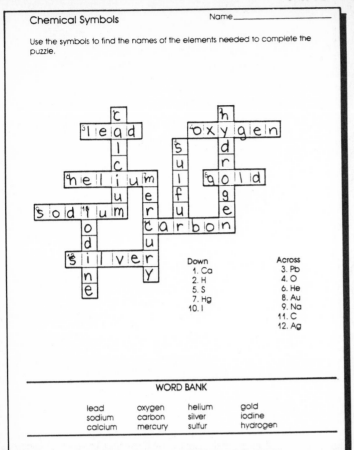

Down
1. Ca
2. H
5. S
7. Hg
10. I

Across
3. Pb
4. O
6. He
8. Au
9. Na
11. C
12. Ag

WORD BANK

lead	oxygen	helium	gold
sodium	carbon	silver	iodine
calcium	mercury	sulfur	hydrogen

Periodic Table of Elements

Name_____

The periodic table can give you a lot of information about each of the elements. Use the **WORD BANK** to label the type of information that the symbols, names and letters represent for each of the elements.

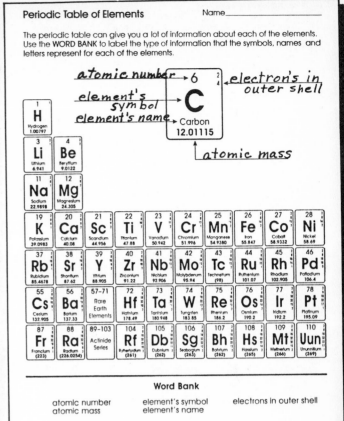

Word Bank

atomic number	element's symbol	electrons in outer shell
atomic mass	element's name	

Atoms

Name_____

Label the parts of the helium atom pictured below.

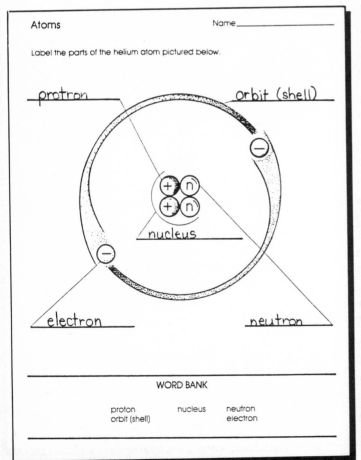

protron

orbit (shell)

nucleus

electron

neutron

WORD BANK

proton	nucleus	neutron
orbit (shell)		electron

Protons, Neutrons and Electrons

Name_____

The atomic number of an atom is the number of protons in each atom of that element. Because atoms are electrically neutral, the atomic number is also the number of electrons. The atomic mass tells the number of protons and neutrons in an atom. By subtracting the atomic number from the atomic mass you can find the number of neutrons.

Complete the chart below.

Atomic number

2
He
Helium
4   K-2

Atomic mass

HELIUM ATOM

atomic mass = 4

atomic number = 2

number of neutrons

4   –   2   =   2

ELEMENT	SYMBOL	ATOMIC NUMBER	ATOMIC MASS	PROTONS	NEUTRONS	ELECTRONS
helium	He	2	4	2	2	2
nitrogen	N	7	14	7	7	7
carbon	C	6	12	6	6	6
sodium	Na	11	23	11	12	11
iron	Fe	26	56	26	30	26
copper	Cu	29	64	29	35	29
silver	Ag	47	108	47	61	47

Answer Key

Name That Molecule!

Name_____

Write the chemical formula for each molecule pictured below.

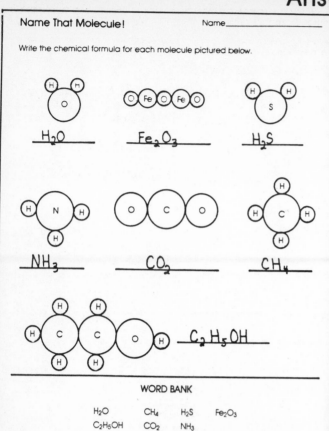

H_2O

Fe_2O_3

H_2S

NH_3

CO_2

CH_4

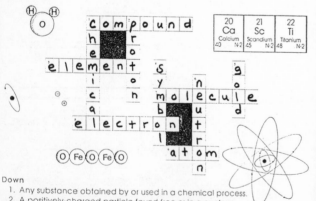

C_2H_5OH

WORD BANK

H_2O	CH_4	H_2S	Fe_2O_3
C_2H_5OH	CO_2	NH_3	

Page 13

Chemical Formulas

Name_____

A chemical formula is a shorthand way to write the name of a compound. Complete the chart below for each of the formulas.

	Compound	Formula	Elements
1.	sodium chloride	NaCl	sodium, chlorine
2.	hydrochloric acid	HCl	hydrogen, chlorine
3.	sodium hydroxide	NaOH	sodium, oxygen, hydrogen
4.	water	H_2O	hydrogen, oxygen
5.	carbon dioxide	CO_2	carbon, oxygen
6.	sulfuric acid	H_2SO_4	hydrogen, sulfur, oxygen
7.	copper sulfate	$CuSO_4$	copper, sulfur, oxygen
8.	alcohol	C_2H_5OH	carbon, hydrogen, oxygen

WORD BANK

sodium chloride	hydrochloric acid	sodium hydroxide
water	oxygen	carbon dioxide
sulfuric acid	copper sulfate	alcohol
sodium	chlorine	hydrogen
copper	sulfur	carbon

Page 14

Chemicals

Name _____

Use what you have learned about chemicals to complete this puzzle. You may need to refer to your science book or encyclopedia.

Across
1. A substance that contains two or more chemical elements.
3. A simple substance made of one type of atom.
7. The smallest particle that displays the physical and chemical properties of a compound.
8. A negatively-charged particle that orbits the nucleus of an atom.
9. What everything is made of; the smallest unit of an element.

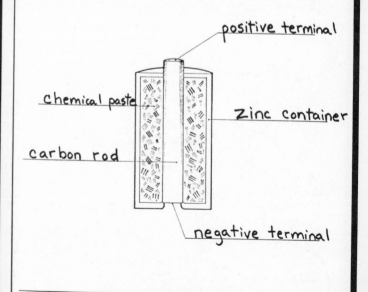

Down
1. Any substance obtained by or used in a chemical process.
2. A positively-charged particle found free or in a nucleus.
4. It stands for the name of an element.
5. **Au** is the symbol for _____.
6. A particle in an atom or by itself with no electrical charge.

WORD BANK

compound	proton	symbol	neutron	chemical
electron	atom	element	gold	molecule

Page 15

Dry Cells

Name _____

The dry cell is a source of portable power used in flashlights, toys, and radios. There are three basic kinds of dry cells that are commonly used—carbon-zinc, alkaline, and mercury.

Label the parts of this carbon-zinc dry cell illustration.

positive terminal

chemical paste

zinc container

carbon rod

negative terminal

WORD BANK

positive terminal	zinc container	chemical paste
negative terminal	carbon rod	

Page 16

Answer Key

Light Bulb

Name _____

Label the parts of the incandescent light bulb pictured below.

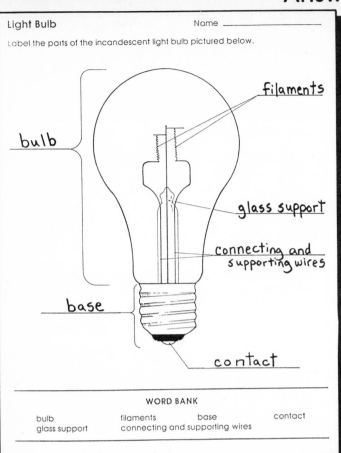

bulb

filaments

glass support

connecting and supporting wires

base

contact

WORD BANK

bulb	filaments	base	contact
glass support	connecting and supporting wires		

Circuits and Switches

Name _____

To be useful electricity must flow in a circuit. Electric circuits can be illustrated with the help of symbols.

Identify the symbols shown here.

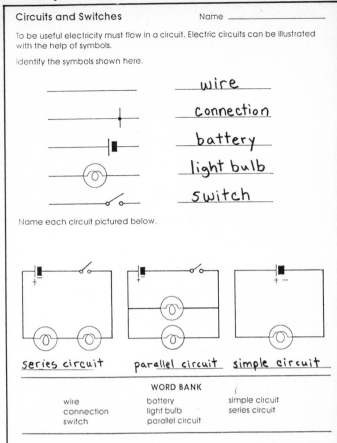

wire

connection

battery

light bulb

switch

Name each circuit pictured below.

series circuit   parallel circuit   simple circuit

WORD BANK

wire	battery	simple circuit
connection	light bulb	series circuit
switch	parallel circuit	

Drawing Electrical Circuits

Name _____

There are three types of simple electrical circuits: a closed circuit, a parallel circuit, and a series circuit. Each type can be set up in more than one way.

Draw lines to show where the wires should connect to make the following circuits.

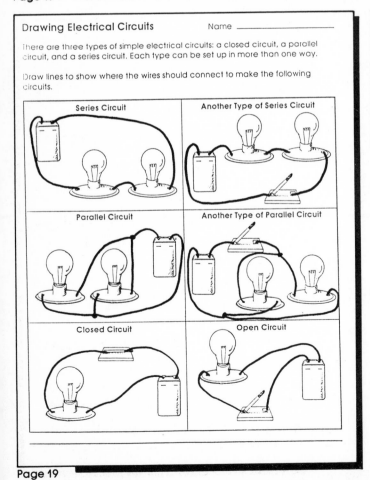

Series Circuit   Another Type of Series Circuit

Parallel Circuit   Another Type of Parallel Circuit

Closed Circuit   Open Circuit

Classy Levers

Name _____

Three classes of levers are pictured below. Label each class of lever and the three lever parts.

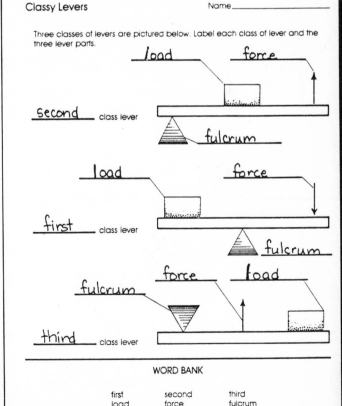

load   force

Second _____ class lever

fulcrum

load   force

first _____ class lever

fulcrum

force   load

fulcrum

third _____ class lever

WORD BANK

first	second	third
load	force	fulcrum

Answer Key

Practical Levers

Name_____

In the space under each picture below write <u>first, second</u> or <u>third</u> to tell the class of the lever.

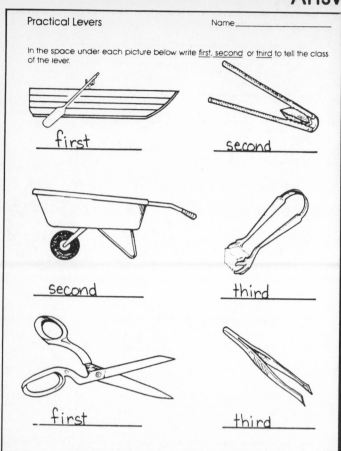

first

second

second

third

first

third

Special Inclined Planes

Name_____

Some simple machines are pictured below. Some of these simple machines are special inclined planes, called wedges and screws. Put an "X" on the simple machines that are not special inclined planes. Label the special inclined planes either <u>screw</u> or <u>wedge</u>.

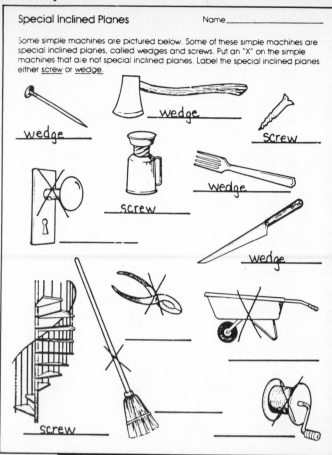

wedge

wedge

screw

screw

wedge

wedge

screw

Pedal Power

Name_____

Your bicycle is a combination of many simple machines. Study the bicycle on this page. Circle and label as many simple machines that you can find on the bicycle shown.

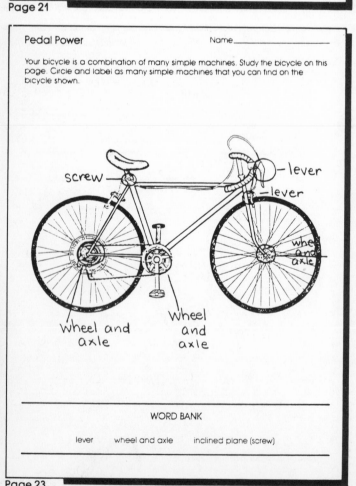

screw

lever

lever

wheel and axle

wheel and axle

wheel and axle

WORD BANK

lever   wheel and axle   inclined plane (screw)

Compound Machines

Name_____

Often two or more simple machines are combined to make one machine called a compound machine. Name the simple machines that are combined to make each of the compound machines pictured below.

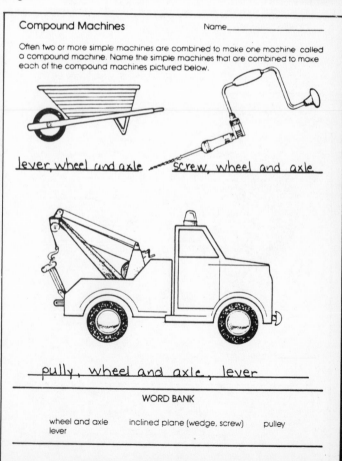

lever, wheel and axle

screw, wheel and axle

pully, wheel and axle, lever

WORD BANK

wheel and axle   inclined plane (wedge, screw)   pulley
lever

Answer Key

The Seasons

Name_____

The diagram below shows the Earth's position in its orbit on four different dates. On the solid line label the equinox dates. On the dotted lines name the season for the Northern Hemisphere.

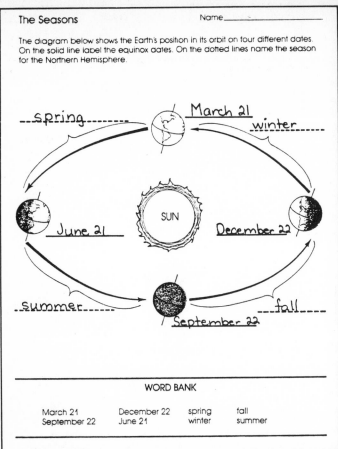

spring   March 21   winter

June 21   SUN   December 22

summer   September 22   fall

WORD BANK

March 21	December 22	spring	fall
September 22	June 21	winter	summer

Summer and Winter

Name_____

The illustration below shows the Earth's position in relation to the Sun for the summer and winter in the Northern Hemisphere. Label the seasons for the Northern Hemisphere, and name the imaginary lines of latitude on the Earth.

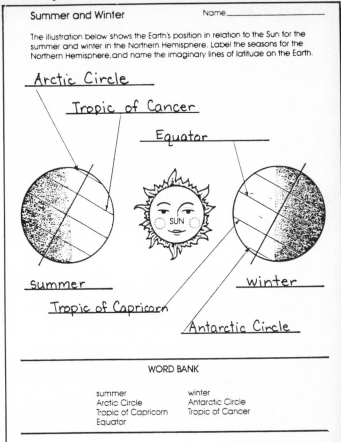

Arctic Circle

Tropic of Cancer

Equator

SUN

summer   winter

Tropic of Capricorn

Antarctic Circle

WORD BANK

summer	winter
Arctic Circle	Antarctic Circle
Tropic of Capricorn	Tropic of Cancer
Equator	

Day and Night

Name_____

Day and night are the result of the Earth's rotation on its axis. Use the words from the WORD BANK to label the illustration below.

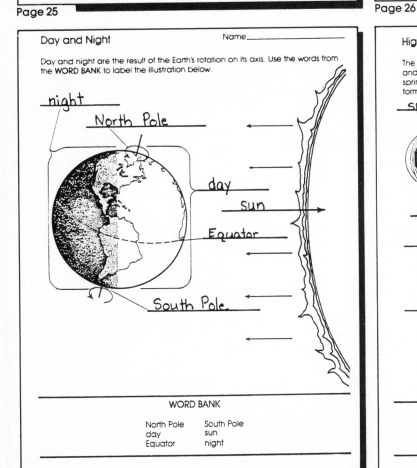

night

North Pole

day

sun

Equator

South Pole

WORD BANK

North Pole	South Pole
day	sun
Equator	night

High Tide

Name_____

The ocean tides are caused mostly by the moon's gravity. When the Sun, moon and Earth line up, the gravitational pull is greatest causing the highest tides, the spring tides. The lowest tides, neap tides, occur when the sun, Earth and moon form right angles. Label the neap tides, spring tides, sun, Earth and moon.

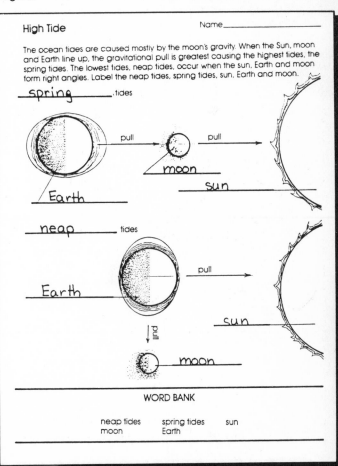

spring   tides

pull   moon   pull

Earth   sun

neap   tides

pull

Earth

sun

pull

moon

WORD BANK

neap tides	spring tides	sun
moon	Earth	

Answer Key

Space Shadows

Name_____

When the sun, moon and Earth are in the proper alignment, either the moon can cast a shadow on the Earth, or the Earth can cast a shadow on the moon. Draw the position of the moon and the shadows for both a lunar and solar eclipse. Label the type of eclipse.

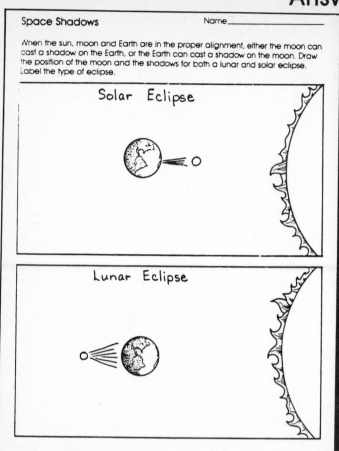

Page 29

Earth Shadow

Name_____

When the sun, Earth and moon are in direct line, the moon moves into the Earth's shadow causing a <u>lunar eclipse</u>. Label the orbits and bodies in the illustration below.

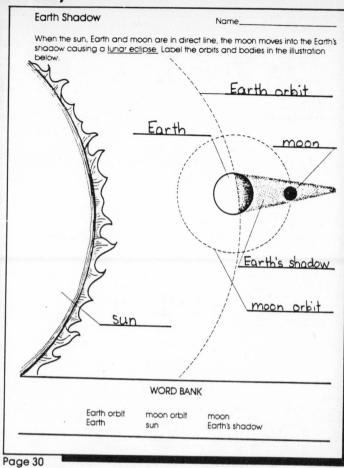

WORD BANK

Earth orbit	moon orbit	moon
Earth	sun	Earth's shadow

Page 30

Moon Shadows

Name_____

When the new moon is directly between the Earth and the sun, an eclipse of the sun occurs. The type of <u>solar eclipse</u> that occurs depends on how much sunlight the moon blocks from the view on Earth. Label the three kinds of solar eclipse. Label the moon, sun and Earth.

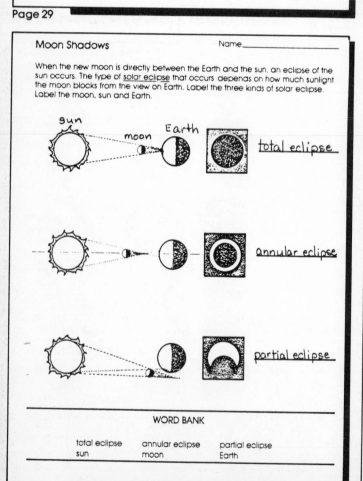

WORD BANK

total eclipse	annular eclipse	partial eclipse
sun	moon	Earth

Page 31

Changing Faces

Name_____

As the moon revolves around the Earth, we can see different amounts of the moon's lighted part. Study the drawing of the moon's different phases and each phase as it would be seen from the Earth. Label each phase.

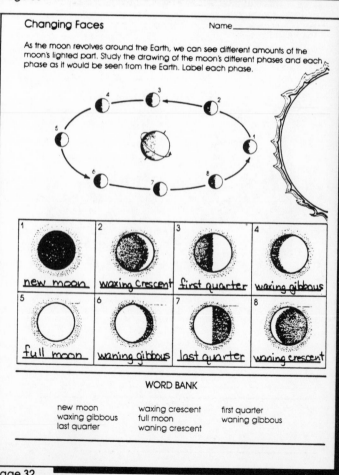

WORD BANK

new moon	waxing crescent	first quarter
waxing gibbous	full moon	waning gibbous
last quarter	waning crescent	

Page 32

Answer Key

Waning and Waxing Moon

Name_____

Use the **WORD BANK** to label the different phases of the moon.

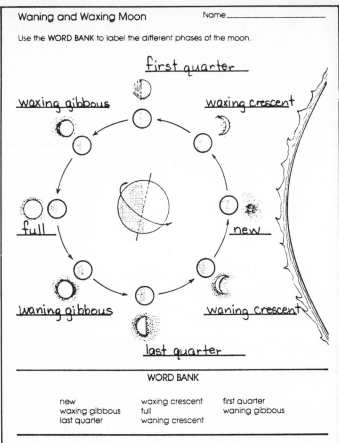

first quarter

waxing gibbous

waxing crescent

full

new

waning gibbous

waning crescent

last quarter

WORD BANK

new	waxing crescent	first quarter
waxing gibbous	full	waning gibbous
last quarter	waning crescent	

Planets of the Solar System

Name_____

All of the planets of the Solar System travel around the sun. Label the planets.

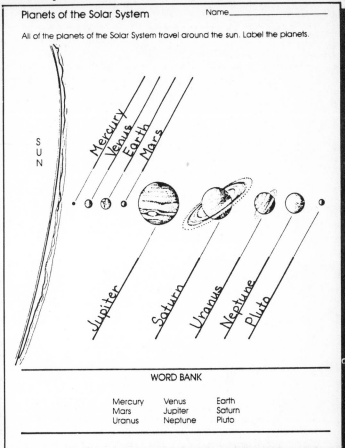

SUN

Mercury
Venus
Earth
Mars

Jupiter
Saturn
Uranus
Neptune
Pluto

WORD BANK

Mercury	Venus	Earth
Mars	Jupiter	Saturn
Uranus	Neptune	Pluto

The Inner Planets

Name_____

The planets that are closest to the sun are called the Inner Planets. Label the Inner Planets and the sun.

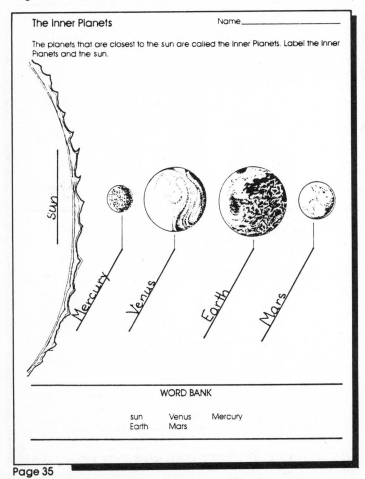

sun

Mercury

Venus

Earth

Mars

WORD BANK

sun	Venus	Mercury
Earth	Mars	

The Outer Planets

Name_____

The planets that are farthest from the sun are called the Outer Planets. Label the Outer Planets.

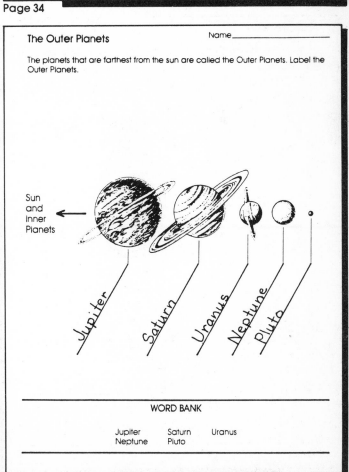

Sun
and
Inner
Planets

Jupiter

Saturn

Uranus

Neptune

Pluto

WORD BANK

Jupiter	Saturn	Uranus
Neptune	Pluto	

Earth Science IF8755   111   © 1991 Instructional Fair, Inc.

Answer Key

Exploring Our Solar System

Name _____

Comets, asteroids, and some meteors travel around the sun in our solar system. But the largest objects traveling around the sun are the planets. Use your science book, encyclopedia, or another source to complete the chart about the planets of our solar system.

Planet	Position From the Sun	Revolution Time (Length of Year — Earth Days)	Rotation Time	Known Satellites	Distance From the Sun
Mercury	1st	88	59 days	0	36 million miles
Venus	2nd	225	243 days	0	67,230,000 miles
Earth	3rd	365	23 hours 56 min.	1	92,960,000 miles
Mars	4th	687	24 hours 37 min.	2	141,700,000 miles
Jupiter	5th	4,333	9 hours 55 min.	16	483,700,000 miles
Saturn	6th	10,759	10 hours 39 min.	20 or more	885,200,000 miles
Uranus	7th	30,685	16 to 28 hours	15	1,781 million miles
Neptune	8th	60,188	18 to 20 hours	8	2,788 million miles
Pluto	9th	90,700	6 days	1	3,660 million miles

Fill in the names of the planets where they belong.

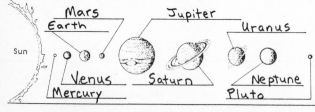

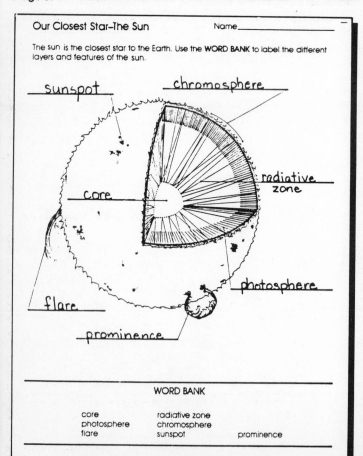

Mars, Earth, Jupiter, Uranus

Sun

Venus, Mercury, Saturn, Neptune, Pluto

Puzzling Planets

Name _____

Use what you have learned about the planets of our solar system to complete the puzzle. You may need to refer to your science book or an encyclopedia.

Across
3. I am the closest in size to the Earth.
4. I am the smallest planet.
6. I have the greatest number of natural satellites.
7. I am the only planet known to support life.
8. I am the Red Planet.
9. I am the most distant planet that can be seen without a telescope.

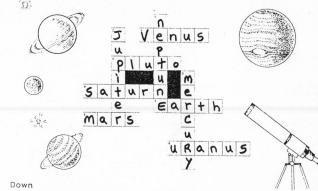

Venus, Pluto, Saturn, Earth, Mars, Uranus (Jupiter, Neptune, Mercury)

Down
1. I am usually the 8th planet from the Sun, but every 248 years I move inside Pluto's orbit for 20 years.
2. I am a large planet known for my "Great Red Spot."
5. I am the closest planet to the Sun.

WORD BANK
Mercury	Venus	Earth
Mars	Jupiter	Saturn
Uranus	Neptune	Pluto

Our Closest Star—The Sun

Name _____

The sun is the closest star to the Earth. Use the **WORD BANK** to label the different layers and features of the sun.

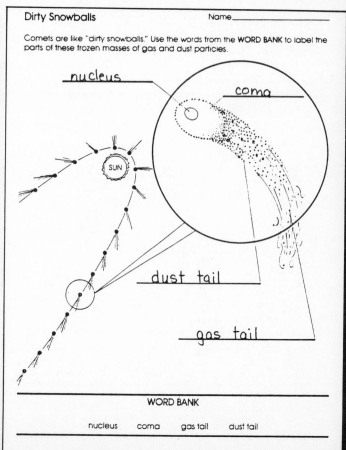

sunspot, chromosphere, radiative zone, core, photosphere, flare, prominence

WORD BANK
core	radiative zone
photosphere	chromosphere
flare	sunspot
	prominence

Dirty Snowballs

Name _____

Comets are like "dirty snowballs." Use the words from the **WORD BANK** to label the parts of these frozen masses of gas and dust particles.

nucleus, coma, dust tail, gas tail

SUN

WORD BANK
nucleus	coma	gas tail	dust tail

Answer Key

The Asteroid Belt

Name_____

Scientists believe that asteroids may be pieces of a planet that was torn apart millions of years ago. Thousands of large asteroids have been tracked, but hundreds of thousands of smaller asteroids are in the asteroid belt.
Label the asteroid belt and the planets in the illustration below.

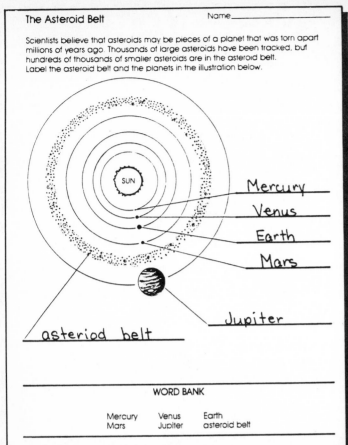

Mercury
Venus
Earth
Mars
Jupiter
asteroid belt

WORD BANK

Mercury	Venus	Earth
Mars	Jupiter	asteroid belt

Page 41

The North Star

Name_____

Because the Earth rotates, all the stars in the sky appear to move from east to west. Because Polaris is directly above the North Pole it does not move, and so it is also called the North Star.

Polaris is found in the constellation Ursa Minor, also called the Little Dipper. The Big Dipper is found in the constellation Ursa Major, also called the Great Bear.
Trace the Big Dipper and Little Dipper. Label Polaris.

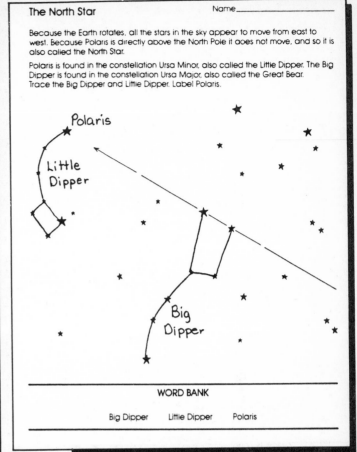

Polaris
Little Dipper
Big Dipper

WORD BANK

Big Dipper   Little Dipper   Polaris

Page 42

Pictures in the Night Sky

Name _____

For thousands of years people from every culture have gazed into the night sky and imagined groups of stars outlining a picture. These star pictures, called constellations, are like giant dot-to-dot puzzles in the night sky.

Name these well-known constellations.

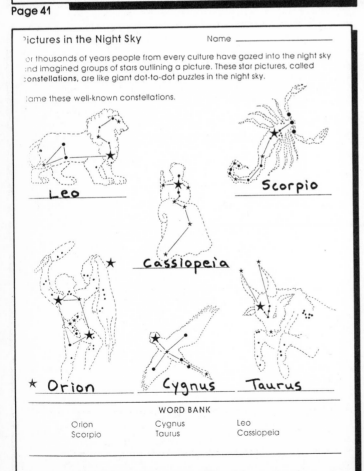

Leo
Scorpio
Cassiopeia
Orion
Cygnus
Taurus

WORD BANK

Orion	Cygnus	Leo
Scorpio	Taurus	Cassiopeia

Page 43

Galaxies

Name_____

Beyond our galaxy lie billions of other galaxies. Use the **WORD BANK** to label the shapes of some of these galaxies.

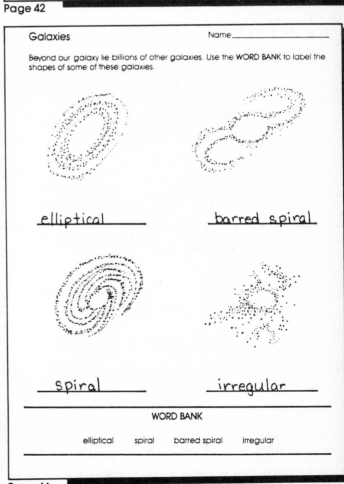

elliptical
barred spiral
spiral
irregular

WORD BANK

elliptical   spiral   barred spiral   irregular

Page 44

Earth Science IF8755

113

© 1991 Instructional Fair, Inc.

Answer Key

Radio Telescope

Name_____

Radio telescopes give us much information about the universe that other kinds of telescopes can't give. Label the parts of the radio telescope.

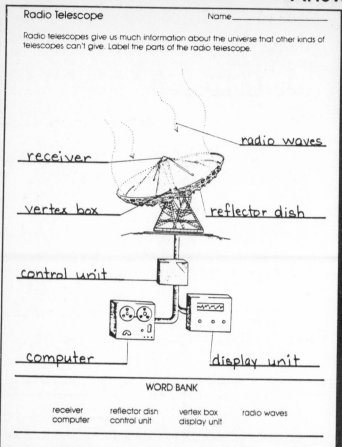

radio waves

receiver

vertex box

reflector dish

control unit

computer

display unit

WORD BANK

receiver reflector dish vertex box radio waves
computer control unit display unit

Page 45

"Optic Glass"

Name_____

In 1609 the Italian astronomer, Galileo, was the first person to see the heavenly bodies closer than they really were with his "optic glass," or telescope. Label the refractor and reflector telescopes and their parts. Use the words from the WORD BANK. You may have to use some of the words more than one time.

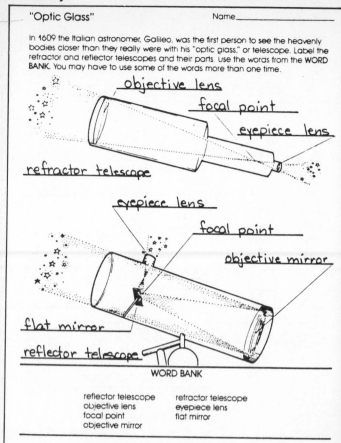

objective lens

focal point

eyepiece lens

refractor telescope

eyepiece lens

focal point

objective mirror

flat mirror

reflector telescope

WORD BANK

reflector telescope   refractor telescope
objective lens   eyepiece lens
focal point   flat mirror
objective mirror

Page 46

The Space Shuttle

Name_____

Use the words in the WORD BANK to label the parts of the Space Shuttle.

reaction control jets

cockpit

orbital maneuvering system engine

rudder and speed brake

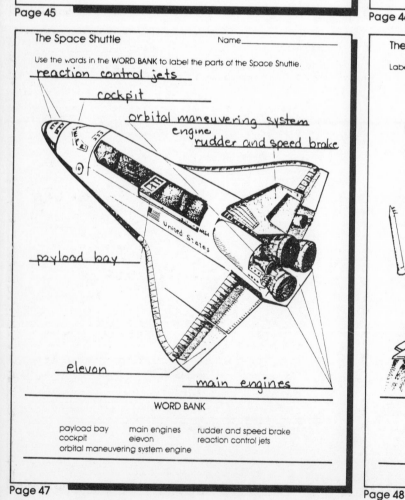

payload bay

elevon

main engines

WORD BANK

payload bay   main engines   rudder and speed brake
cockpit   elevon   reaction control jets
orbital maneuvering system engine

Page 47

The Flight of the Space Shuttle

Name_____

Label the different phases of the Space Shuttle's mission.

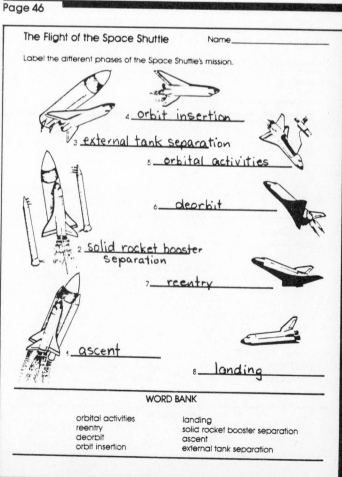

4. orbit insertion

3. external tank separation

5. orbital activities

6. deorbit

2. solid rocket booster separation

7. reentry

1. ascent

8. landing

WORD BANK

orbital activities   landing
reentry   solid rocket booster separation
deorbit   ascent
orbit insertion   external tank separation

Page 48

Answer Key

Space Shuttle Launch Site

Name_____

Label the parts of the Space Shuttle's launch site using the words from the WORD BANK.

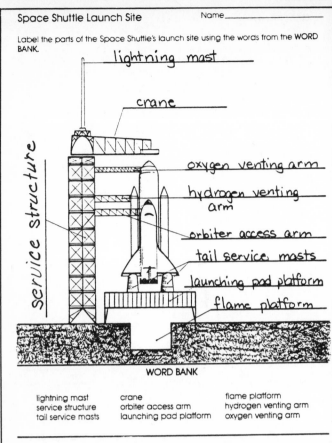

- lightning mast
- crane
- oxygen venting arm
- hydrogen venting arm
- orbiter access arm
- tail service masts
- launching pad platform
- flame platform
- service structure

WORD BANK

lightning mast	crane	flame platform
service structure	orbiter access arm	hydrogen venting arm
tail service masts	launching pad platform	oxygen venting arm

Hemispheres

Name_____

The Earth is a giant sphere. When the Earth is divided into two equal parts each part is called a hemisphere. Label the four hemispheres pictured below using the words from the WORD BANK.

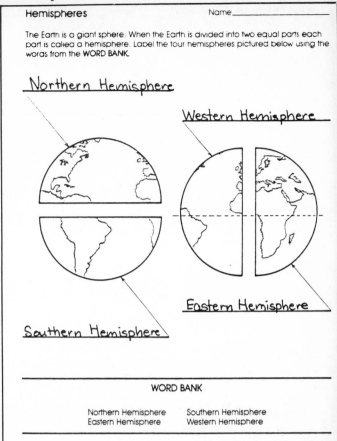

Northern Hemisphere

Western Hemisphere

Eastern Hemisphere

Southern Hemisphere

WORD BANK

Northern Hemisphere	Southern Hemisphere
Eastern Hemisphere	Western Hemisphere

More Than One Hemisphere

Name_____

You live in more than one hemisphere. Although it's impossible to live in the Northern and Southern Hemispheres, or the Eastern and Western Hemisphere at the same time, it is possible to live in the Northern and Eastern, or Northern and Western, or Southern and Eastern, or Southern and Western Hemisphere. Label the two hemispheres pictured in each hemisphere.

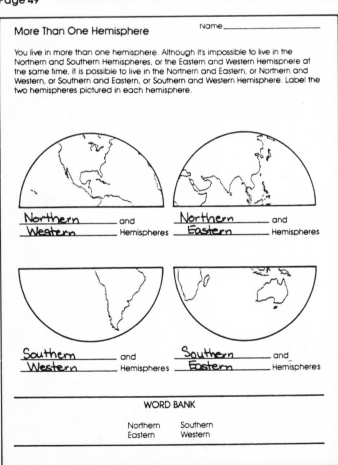

Northern and Western Hemispheres

Northern and Eastern Hemispheres

Southern and Western Hemispheres

Southern and Eastern Hemispheres

WORD BANK

Northern	Southern
Eastern	Western

Map Features

Name_____

Everyone from the weather forecaster to a family on vacation finds maps as very valuable tools. But they are useful only if you know how to use their many features. Label the parts of the map below. Then explain the purpose of each.

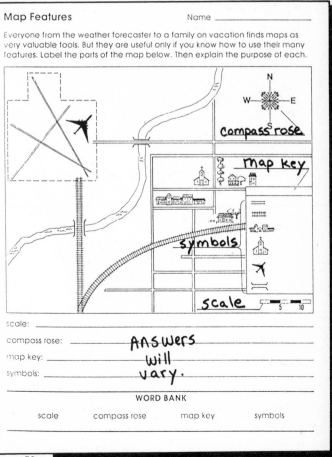

compass rose

map key

symbols

scale

scale: _____

compass rose: _____ Answers

map key: _____ will

symbols: _____ vary.

WORD BANK

scale	compass rose	map key	symbols

Earth Science IF8755   115   © 1991 Instructional Fair, Inc.

Answer Key

Using Latitude and Longitude

Name _____

Use the latitude and longitude grid to pinpoint each location specified in the questions below.

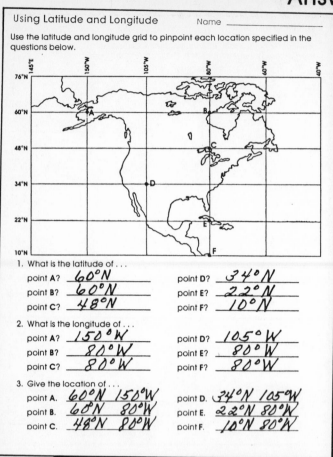

1. What is the latitude of . . .

point A? **60°N**	point D? **34°N**
point B? **60°N**	point E? **22°N**
point C? **48°N**	point F? **10°N**

2. What is the longitude of . . .

point A? **150°W**	point D? **105°W**
point B? **80°W**	point E? **80°W**
point C? **80°W**	point F? **80°W**

3. Give the location of . . .

point A. **60°N 150°W**	point D. **34°N 105°W**
point B. **60°N 80°W**	point E. **22°N 80°W**
point C. **48°N 80°W**	point F. **10°N 80°W**

Page 53

Sea of Air

Name _____

Our atmosphere extends several hundred kilometers upward. In the illustration below notice different layers of the atmosphere and what may be found in those layers. Label each of the layers and objects found in these layers using the words from the WORD BANK.

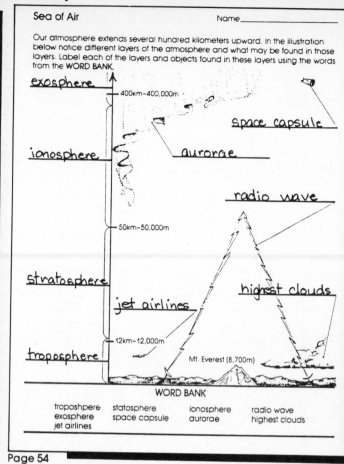

exosphere — 400km-400,000m
space capsule
ionosphere — aurorae
radio wave
50km-50,000m
stratosphere — highest clouds
jet airlines
troposphere — 12km-12,000m
Mt. Everest (8,700m)

WORD BANK

troposhpere	statosphere	ionosphere	radio wave
exosphere	space capsule	aurorae	highest clouds
jet airlines			

Page 54

The Center of the Earth

Name _____

The Earth has four layers. Color the layers of the Earth and the key.

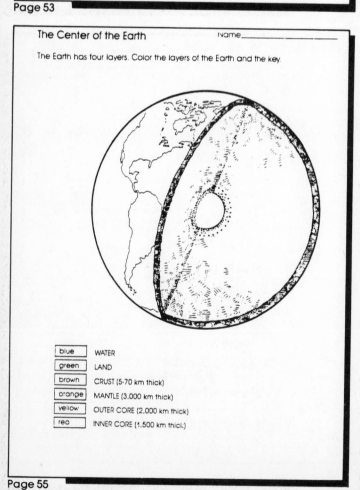

blue	WATER
green	LAND
brown	CRUST (5-70 km thick)
orange	MANTLE (3,000 km thick)
yellow	OUTER CORE (2,000 km thick)
red	INNER CORE (1,500 km thick)

Page 55

Solid to the Core

Name _____

If you could take a slice out of the Earth you would find that it has four layers. Label each of these layers.

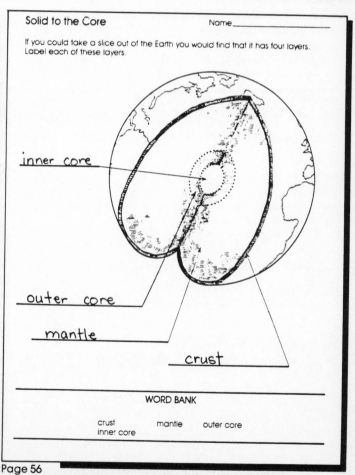

inner core

outer core

mantle

crust

WORD BANK

crust   mantle   outer core
inner core

Page 56

Earth Science IF8755

116

© 1991 Instructional Fair, Inc.

Answer Key

The Rock Cycle

Name _____

With the help of heat, pressure, and weathering, one kind of rock can be changed into a new kind of rock. For example, beautiful marble is formed from limestone, and slate comes from shale and clay.

The changing of rocks is an ongoing cycle. There is no true beginning, but it might be easier to understand by beginning with magma. Complete the rock cycle diagram pictured below.

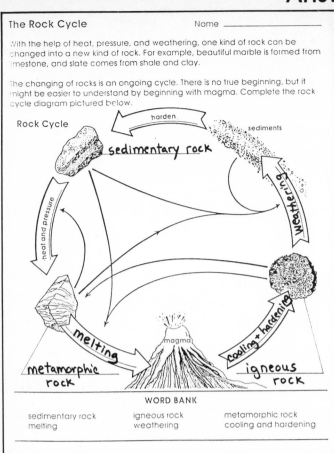

Rock Cycle

harden

sedimentary rock

sediments

weathering

heat and pressure

melting

metamorphic rock

magma

cooling + hardening

igneous rock

WORD BANK

sedimentary rock	igneous rock	metamorphic rock
melting	weathering	cooling and hardening

Soil Profile

Name _____

Study the soil profile pictured below. Identify the layer or layers where each of the following is found.

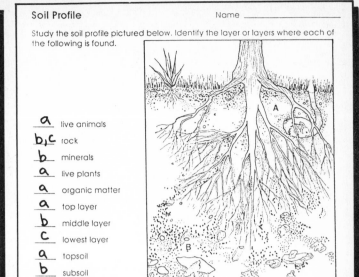

- **a** live animals
- **b,c** rock
- **b** minerals
- **a** live plants
- **a** organic matter
- **a** top layer
- **b** middle layer
- **c** lowest layer
- **a** topsoil
- **b** subsoil
- **a,b** tree roots
- **c** boulders

Making Crystals

Name _____

People have always been fascinated by the incredible beauty of crystals. Crystals come in a wide variety of shapes.

Cut out each of the crystal patterns on the solid line. Then fold along the dotted lines. Tape the sides together. Match the common crystal shapes drawn here with the ones you have created.

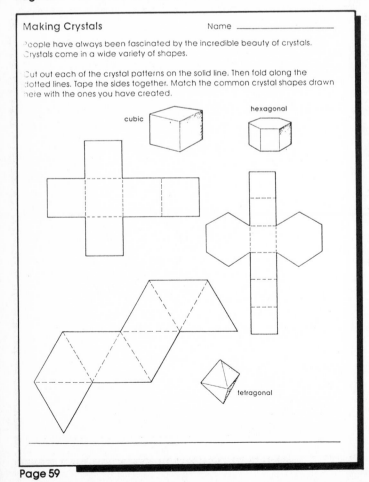

cubic

hexagonal

tetragonal

Mohs Hardness Scale

Name _____

One of the most useful properties used for identification of a mineral is its hardness. The Mohs hardness scale measures a mineral's hardness by means of a simple scratch test.

Name the mineral that belongs in each step of the Mohs Hardness Scale chart.

Mohs Hardness Scale		
Hardness	Mineral	Common Tests
1	Talc	Fingernail will scratch it.
2	Gypsum	
3	Calcite	Fingernail will not scratch it; a copper penny will.
4	Fluorite	Knife blade or window glass will scratch it.
5	Apatite	
6	Feldspar/Orthoclase	
7	Quartz	Will scratch a steel knife or window glass.
8	Topaz	
9	Corundum	
10	Diamond	Will scratch all common materials.

WORD BANK

Talc	diamond	Gypsum	Corundum
Calcite	Topaz	Fluorite	Quartz
Apatite	Feldspar/Orthoclase		

Name That Mineral

Name _____

One can identify many minerals by carefully observing their physical characteristics. **Some** of these characteristics are:

Hardness — This is determined with a scratch test.
Color — Color depends on the substances that make up the crystals. Varies greatly.
Luster — This refers to how light reflects off the mineral.

Enough information has been given to you here to help you find the unknown minerals and fill in the chart.

Hardness Scale

Hardness	Mineral	Common Tests
1	Talc	Fingernail will scratch it.
2	Gypsum/ Kaolinite	
3	Mica/ Calcite	A copper penny will scratch it.
4	Fluorite	Knife blade or window glass will scratch it.
5	Apatite/ Hornblende	
6	Feldspar	
7	Quartz	Will scratch a steel knife or window glass.
8	Topaz	
9	Corundum	
10	Diamond	Will scratch all common materials.

Color	Mineral
White:	Quartz, Feldspar, Calcite, Kaolinite, Talc
Yellow:	Quartz, Kaolinite
Black:	Hornblende, Mica
Gray:	Feldspar, Gypsum
Colorless:	Quartz, Calcite, Gypsum

Luster	Mineral
Glassy:	Quartz, Feldspar, Hornblende
Pearly:	Mica, Gypsum, Talc
Dull:	Kaolinite

THE UNKNOWN MINERALS —

Hardness	Color	Luster	Mineral
Will scratch a steel knife or window glass.	yellow	glassy	Quartz
Will scratch a steel knife or window glass.	gray	glassy	Feldspar
A copper penny will scratch it.	black	pearly	Mica
Fingernail will scratch it.	white	pearly	Talc
Knife blade or window glass will scratch it.	black	glassy	Hornblende

Page 61

Classy Rocks

Name _____

There are three main groups of rock: **igneous** rock, **metamorphic** rock, and **sedimentary** rock. Each of the rocks pictured on this page belongs to one of these groups. Fill in the definitions. Then, in the space below each picture, tell which group each rock belongs to.

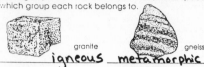

granite — **igneous** gneiss — **metamorphic** marble — **metamorphic**

limestone — **sedimentary** shale — **sedimentary** basalt — **igneous**

sandstone — **sedimentary** slate — **metamorphic** obsidian — **igneous**

conglomerate — **sedimentary**

Kind of Rock	Definition
Igneous	cooled magma
Sedimentary	layers of loose material, etc.
Metamorphic	rock that has been changed etc.

WORD BANK	DEFINITIONS
igneous	layers of loose material which solidified
metamorphic	cooled magma
sedimentary	rock that has been changed into a new rock

Page 62

Rocks and Minerals

Name _____

Use what you have learned about rocks and minerals to complete this puzzle.

Across
2. An uneven break
3. Substance with 3-dimensional plane faces
4. Feel of a surface when rubbed
6. Measured with Mohs Scale
8. Quartz is an example of a _____ .

f r a c t u r e
c r y s t a l
t e x t u r e
g h a r d n e s s
m i n e r a l

(Down words: luster, cleavage, gem, streak)

Down
1. Light reflected from a mineral's surface
3. Smooth break in a mineral
5. Large mineral crystal with brilliant color
7. A _____ test shows the color of a mineral when it is rubbed into a fine powder.

WORD BANK

hardness	crystal	streak
gem	cleavage	texture
fracture	luster	mineral

Page 63

Whose Fault Is It?

Name _____

A crack in the Earth's bedrock is called a fault. There are two types of faults, the strike-slip fault and the dip-slip fault.
California is known for the San Andreas Fault. Draw the San Andreas Fault on the map of California, then label the two different kinds of faults.

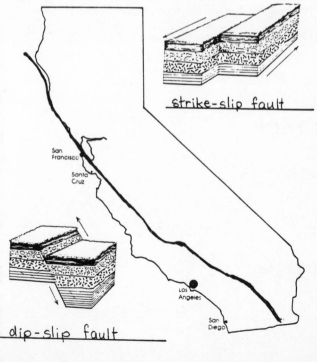

strike-slip fault

San Francisco
Santa Cruz

Los Angeles
San Diego

dip-slip fault

Page 64

Answer Key

Drifting Continents

Name_____

About 250 million years ago there was one continent called Pangaea (Figure A). By 45 million years ago the land mass split into seven land masses (Figure B). Label the land masses in Figure B.

Figure A

Figure B

India
Eurasia
Africa
North America
South America
Antarctica
Australia

WORD BANK

North America	South America	Eurasia
Africa	India	Australia
Antarctica		

"Broken Plates"

Name_____

Below are puzzle pieces of the Earth's seven major plates. Cut out the plates and glue them on a separate sheet of paper. Label the plates.

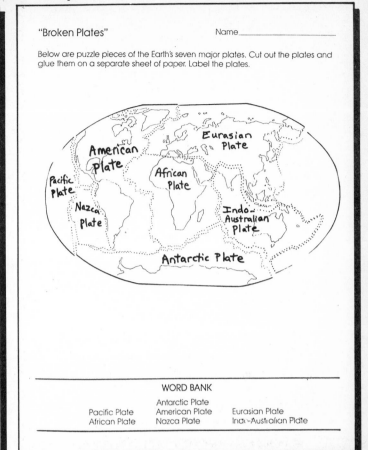

American Plate
Eurasian Plate
Pacific Plate
African Plate
Nazca Plate
Indo-Australian Plate
Antarctic Plate

WORD BANK

	Antarctic Plate	
Pacific Plate	American Plate	Eurasian Plate
African Plate	Nazca Plate	Indo-Australian Plate

Earth's Moving Plates

Name _____

The Earth's crust is made of rigid plates that are always moving. The boundaries of some of these plates are along the edges of the continents, while others are in the middle of the ocean. The map on this page shows the major plates near North and South America.

Using an encyclopedia or some other source, label the eight plates pictured below.

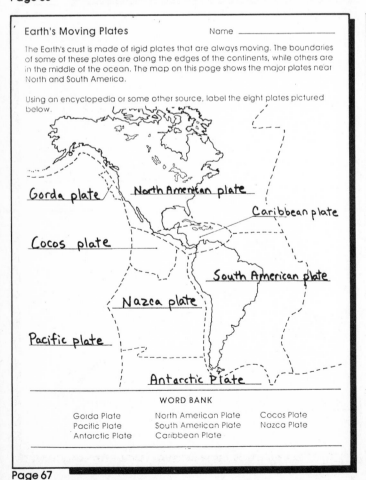

Gorda plate
North American plate
Caribbean plate
Cocos plate
South American plate
Nazca plate
Pacific plate
Antarctic Plate

WORD BANK

Gorda Plate	North American Plate	Cocos Plate
Pacific Plate	South American Plate	Nazca Plate
Antarctic Plate	Caribbean Plate	

Bending the Earth's Crust

Name _____

According to the theory of plate tectonics, the earth's crust is broken into about twenty plates. These plates are slowly moving. The edges of some of these plates are moving toward each other. A trench is formed when one plate bends and dives under another. The diving edge then descends into the earth's hot, mantle and starts melting into magma. The magma can then rise and break through the earth's crust and burst out of a volcano. The edge of the above-riding plate crumples, resulting in a mountain range.

Label the diagram below.

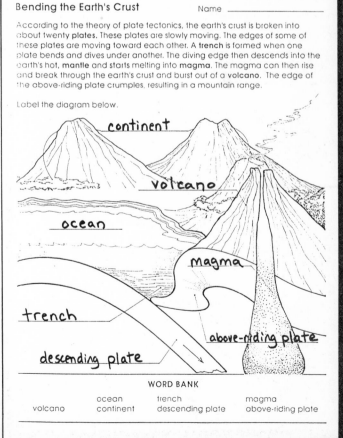

continent
volcano
ocean
magma
trench
above-riding plate
descending plate

WORD BANK

	ocean	trench	magma
volcano	continent	descending plate	above-riding plate

Answer Key

Volcanoes

Name_____

Label the parts of this volcano using the words from the WORD BANK.

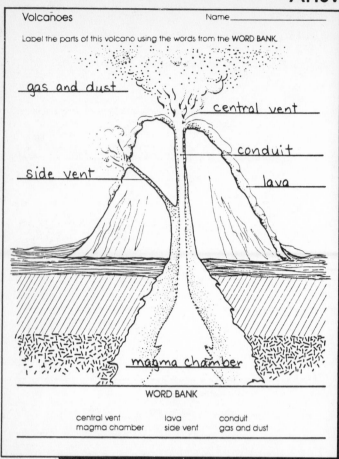

- gas and dust
- central vent
- conduit
- side vent
- lava
- magma chamber

WORD BANK

| central vent | lava | conduit |
| magma chamber | side vent | gas and dust |

Page 69

"Ring of Fire"

Name_____

There are more than 500 active volcanoes in the world. More than half of these encircle the Pacific Ocean in an area called the "Ring of Fire." Color the region known as the "Ring of Fire." Research this region, locate and label some of its well-known volcanoes.

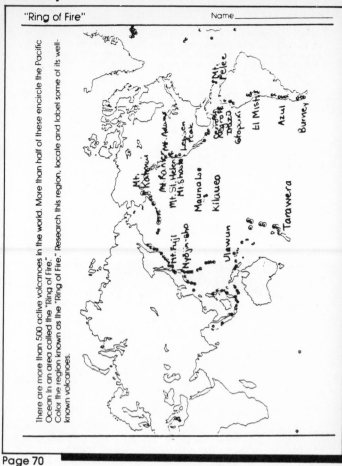

Page 70

Volcanic Cones

Name_____

Volcanic cones can be classified by their shapes. Label the three different kinds of volcanic cones pictured below. Label the parts of the volcanoes.

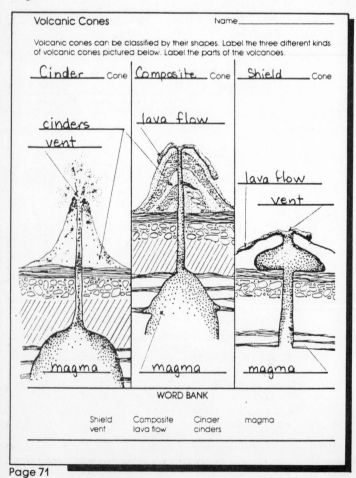

Cinder Cone — cinders, vent, magma

Composite Cone — lava flow, magma

Shield Cone — lava flow, vent, magma

WORD BANK

| Shield | Composite | Cinder | magma |
| vent | lava flow | cinders | |

Page 71

Forming Igneous Rock

Name_____

Igneous rock is one of the three major types of rock. It is formed by the hardening of molten rock (magma). Magma does not always reach the Earth's surface as lava erupting from a volcano. It often forms other igneous rock structures underground.

Label the igneous rock structures shown here.

- lava
- volcano
- dike
- laccolith
- sill
- batholith

WORD BANK

| laccolith | sill | dike | batholith |
| lava | volcano | | |

Page 72

Answer Key

Drilling for Oil

Name _____

Most oil is found thousands of feet beneath the surface of the earth. It is trapped beneath layers of nonporous rock, such as shale, which will not allow the oil to pass through. Often pockets of natural gas will also form where there is oil. Oil companies drill for oil using large drills that grind through the ground and rock.

The illustration below shows one example of where oil can be found. Label the illustration.

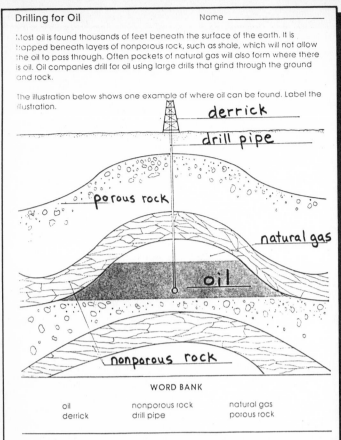

derrick
drill pipe
porous rock
natural gas
oil
nonporous rock

WORD BANK

oil	nonporous rock	natural gas
derrick	drill pipe	porous rock

Coral Reefs

Name _____

Three types of coral reefs are pictured below.
1. Label each type of coral reef.
2. Label the features that are enclosed by the reef.
3. Number the steps in the formation of an atoll.

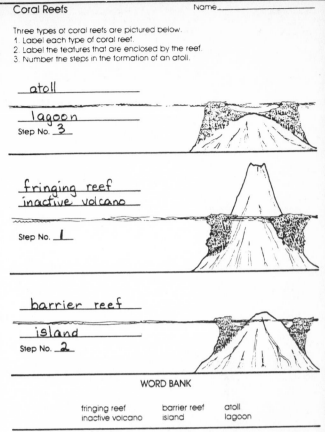

atoll
lagoon
Step No. **3**

fringing reef
inactive volcano

Step No. **1**

barrier reef
island
Step No. **2**

WORD BANK

fringing reef	barrier reef	atoll
inactive volcano	island	lagoon

Groundwater at Work

Name _____

Groundwater is water in the ground that is near the surface. People remove groundwater with wells. Label the pictures below with the terms found in the Word Bank.

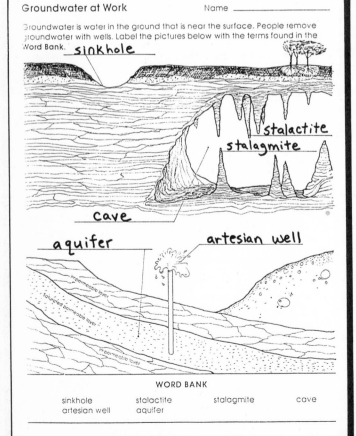

sinkhole
stalactite
stalagmite
cave
aquifer
artesian well

WORD BANK

sinkhole	stalactite	stalagmite	cave
artesian well	aquifer		

The Ocean Floor

Name _____

Label the features of the ocean floor.

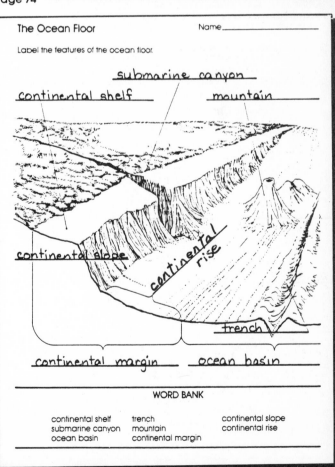

submarine canyon
continental shelf
mountain
continental slope
continental rise
trench
continental margin
ocean basin

WORD BANK

continental shelf	trench	continental slope
submarine canyon	mountain	continental rise
ocean basin	continental margin	

Answer Key

Ocean Currents

Name _____

Water moves within the oceans in streams called currents. Label the ocean currents pictured on the map.

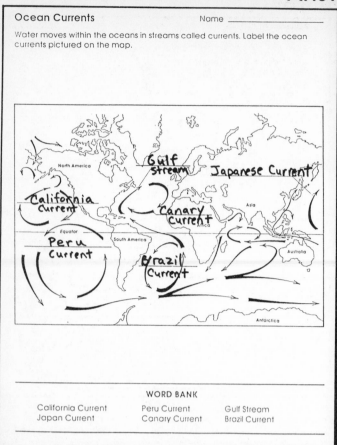

WORD BANK

California Current   Peru Current   Gulf Stream
Japan Current   Canary Current   Brazil Current

Landform Regions of the United States

Name _____

The continental United States can be divided into several major landform regions. Label each region using the list found in the Word Bank.

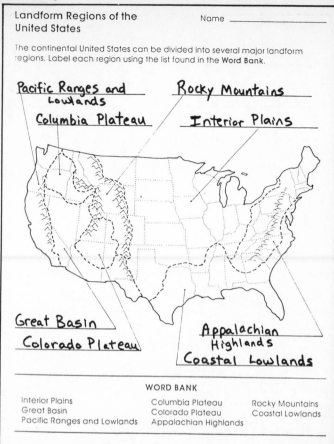

WORD BANK

Interior Plains   Columbia Plateau   Rocky Mountains
Great Basin   Colorado Plateau   Coastal Lowlands
Pacific Ranges and Lowlands   Appalachian Highlands

Topographic Maps

Name _____

A topographic map uses contour lines to show the elevation and slope of hills, valleys, and other natural features. Label the various land features and elements of the topographic map pictured below.

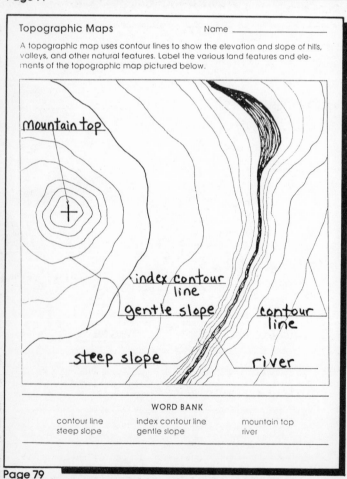

WORD BANK

contour line   index contour line   mountain top
steep slope   gentle slope   river

Benchmark to Benchmark

Name _____

Use the benchmarks on the map below to help you draw the contour lines. The contour lines should be drawn at 20 foot intervals.

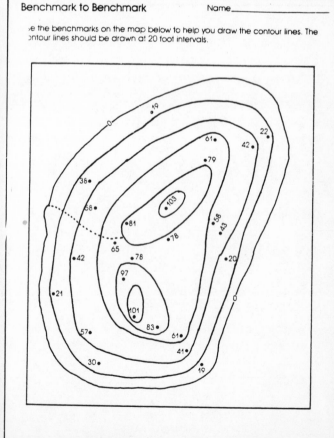

Answer Key

Topographical Maps

Name_____

Topographical maps give the geographical positions and elevations of both manmade and natural features. Using the contour lines and contour intervals, label the elevations of the features on this map.

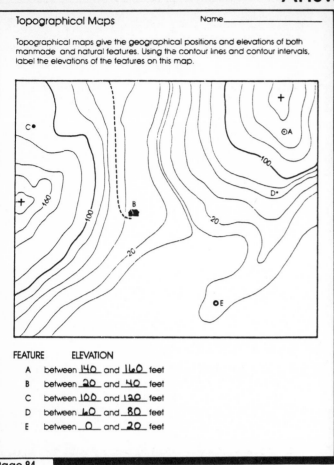

FEATURE	ELEVATION
A	between __140__ and __160__ feet
B	between __20__ and __40__ feet
C	between __100__ and __120__ feet
D	between __60__ and __80__ feet
E	between __0__ and __20__ feet

Page 81

Meandering River

Name_____

A river goes through different stages of development as it erodes its channel. Label the parts of the river.

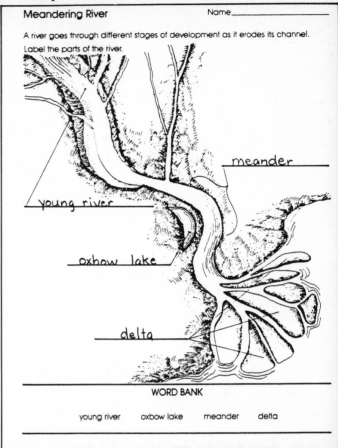

WORD BANK

young river   oxbow lake   meander   delta

Page 82

River System

Name_____

A river may begin its journey to the sea high up in the mountains as a melting glacier, or as a number of small streams and brooks high up in the hills. As the river flows downhill the moving water reshapes the land by carrying away sand, stones, and clay. The river and all the water that flows into it make up the **river system**.

Label the parts of the river system.

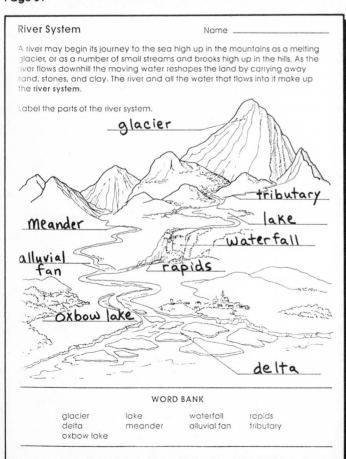

WORD BANK

glacier	lake	waterfall	rapids
delta	meander	alluvial fan	tributary
oxbow lake			

Page 83

Glaciers

Name_____

Tons of ice and trapped rock scrape and grind mountain walls as a glacier creeps down a mountain. The tremendous force of the moving glacier reshapes the mountain slopes in its path, leaving behind deposits of rock.

Label the formations made by the moving glacier.

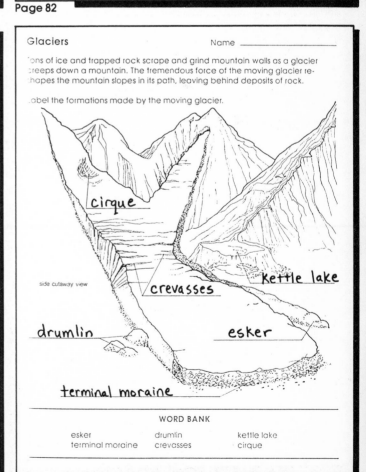

WORD BANK

esker	drumlin	kettle lake
terminal moraine	crevasses	cirque

Page 84

Answer Key

You're All Wet!!!

Name _____

It's a wet day. The symbols on the weather map show eight different forms of precipitation occuring around the country. Label each form of precipitation.

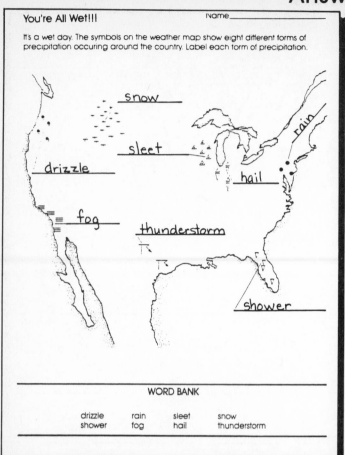

snow
sleet
rain
drizzle
hail
fog
thunderstorm
shower

WORD BANK

drizzle	rain	sleet	snow
shower	fog	hail	thunderstorm

Page 85

Gentle Breezes

Name _____

On the chart below list the wind speed and wind direction for the cities that are listed.

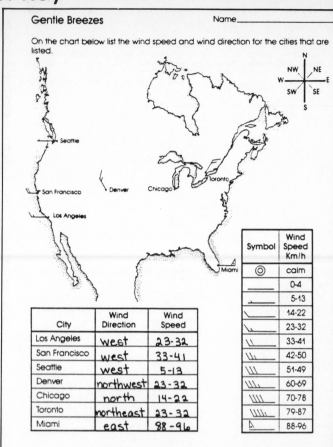

City	Wind Direction	Wind Speed
Los Angeles	west	23-32
San Francisco	west	33-41
Seattle	west	5-13
Denver	northwest	23-32
Chicago	north	14-22
Toronto	northeast	23-32
Miami	east	88-96

Symbol	Wind Speed Km/h
◎	calm
	0-4
	5-13
	14-22
	23-32
	33-41
	42-50
	51-49
	60-69
	70-78
	79-87
	88-96

Page 86

Weather Map Symbols

Name _____

Weather maps, like the one on this page, provide data from which meteorologists prepare weather forecasts. To accurately read a weather map you must be able to understand the weather map symbols.

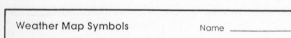

Label each of these weather map symbols.

cold front
warm front
occluded front
stationary front
clear skies
rain
partly cloudy

snow
cloudy
high pressure
low pressure
wind speed and direction
thunderstorm

WORD BANK

rain	clear skies	thunderstorm	cloudy
snow	partly cloudy	cold front	occluded front
high pressure	warm front	stationary front	low pressure
wind speed and direction			

Page 87

Using a Weather Map

Name _____

Weather maps show the recorded weather conditions over a large geographic area. Use the map shown on this page along with what you have learned about weather symbols to complete the chart.

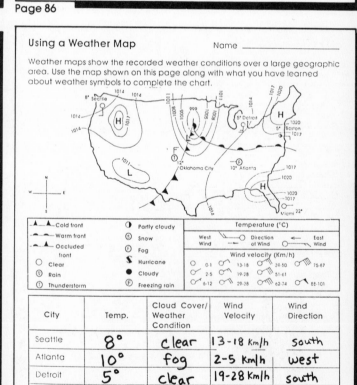

City	Temp.	Cloud Cover/ Weather Condition	Wind Velocity	Wind Direction
Seattle	8°	clear	13-18 Km/h	south
Atlanta	10°	fog	2-5 Km/h	west
Detroit	5°	clear	19-28 Km/h	south
Miami	22°	clear	2-5 Km/h	east
Oklahoma City	12°	thunderstorm	19-28 Km/h	north
Boston	5	partly cloudy	13-18 Km/h	east

Page 88

Answer Key

Precipitation
Name _____

Precipitation is water vapor that condenses and falls to the earth. Depending on the conditions in the atmosphere, precipitation can fall in a number of forms. The symbol for each form is pictured below.

Identify each form of precipitation by drawing its symbol next to its description.

Symbols

rain ⁘

drizzle ⌐

rain showers ● ▽

sleet ⟁

snow ✳

hail ▲

fog ☰

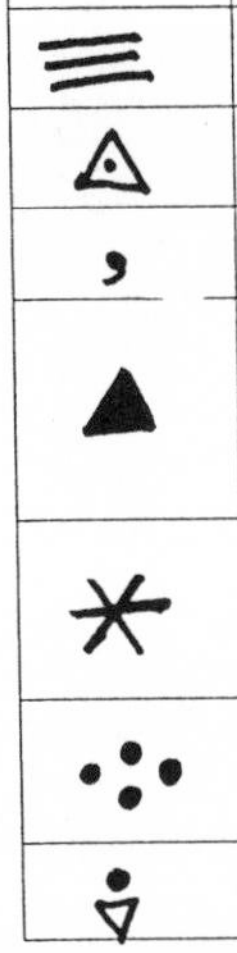

Symbol	Definition
☰	Clouds that form close to the ground.
⟁	Droplets that freeze as they get closer to the ground.
⌐	Light mist of droplets falling to the earth.
▲	Droplets of water freeze around ice crystals as they bounce up and down within a storm cloud. Fall to earth when they get heavy.
✳	Vapor that changes directly into crystalline flakes because of freezing temperatures.
⁘	Water vapor that forms droplets and falls to the earth.
▽	Large amount of droplets falling to the earth.

Use another source to help you complete this chart.

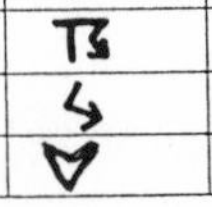

Weather	Symbol	Definition
thunderstorm	T̄S̄	Answers
lightning	ϟ	will
squall	∀	vary.

Page 89

Moving Weather Systems
Name _____

A careful study of the daily weather maps found in your newspaper will show that weather systems are constantly on the move.

You will need four copies of this page. Use a new sheet every day for three days to copy that day's weather pattern (frontal systems, pressure cells, precipitation) from your newspaper. Study the movement of the pattern. Then draw a weather pattern predicting where the weather systems will move on the next day.

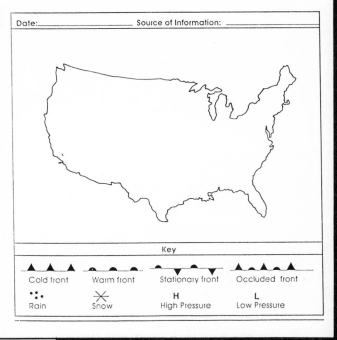

Date: _____ Source of Information: _____

Key

Cold front	Warm front	Stationary front	Occluded front
▲▲▲	◗◗◗	▲◗▲◗	▲◗▲◗

| ⁘ Rain | ✳ Snow | H High Pressure | L Low Pressure |

Page 90

Relative Humidity
Name _____

Relative humidity is the amount of water vapor that the air can hold at a certain temperature. Relative humidity is measured with a hygrometer.
Use the table to find the relative humidity for the data recorded on the chart below.

Day	Dry Temp.	Wet Temp.	Relative Humidity
Mon.	22°	21°	92 %
Tue.	23°	21°	84 %
Wed.	21°	19°	83 %
Thur.	19°	18°	91 %
Fri.	18°	15°	73 %
Sat.	19°	15°	65 %
Sun.	17°	13°	64 %

Dry bulb temp. °C	Difference between wet and dry temperatures							
	1°	2°	3°	4°	5°	6°	7°	8°
15°	90	80	71	61	53	44	36	27
16°	90	81	71	63	54	46	38	30
17°	90	81	72	64	55	47	40	32
18°	91	82	73	65	57	49	41	34
19°	91	82	74	65	58	50	43	36
20°	91	83	74	66	59	51	44	37
21°	91	83	75	67	60	53	46	39
22°	92	83	76	68	61	54	47	40
23°	92	84	76	69	62	55	48	42
24°	92	84	77	69	62	56	49	43
25°	92	84	77	70	63	57	50	44
26°	92	85	78	71	64	58	51	46
27°	92	85	78	71	65	58	52	47

Use your data to make a graph of the relative humidity.

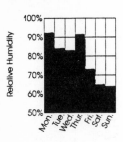

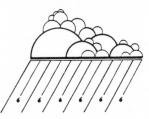

Page 91

Air Currents
Name _____

Name the three air current phenomena pictured below using words from the Word Bank. Then fill in each explanation.

This picture shows: the Coriolis effect
Explanation: The earth's rotation affects the paths of winds.

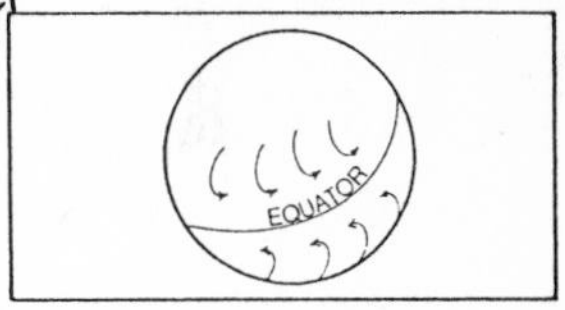

This picture shows: a land breeze
Explanation: At night, cool air over shore replaces warm air over sea.

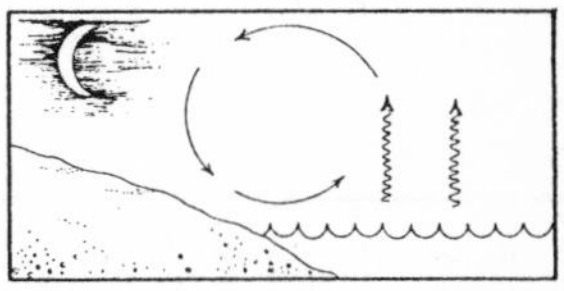

This picture shows: a sea breeze
Explanation: During day, cooler air from sea replaces warm air over shore.

WORD BANK	EXPLANATIONS
a land breeze	The earth's rotation affects the paths of winds.
a sea breeze	During day, cooler air from sea replaces warm air over shore.
the Coriolis effect	At night, cool air over shore replaces warm air over sea.

Page 92

125

Answer Key

The Water Cycle

Name _____

The never-ending circulation of the waters of the earth from the oceans, to the air, and to the land is called the water cycle. Label the three major steps in the water cycle. Then explain how the water cycle works in your own words.

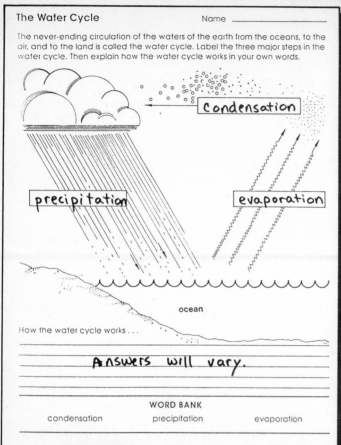

How the water cycle works . . .

Answers will vary.

WORD BANK

condensation   precipitation   evaporation

What's Up Front?

Name_____

A front is where two air masses meet. Changes in the weather take place along a front.

Label the two fronts and the kinds of air masses in the illustrations below.

cold ___ front   cold air mass   warm air mass

warm air mass   cold air mass   warm ___ front

Label the four kinds of fronts that are represented by the symbols below.

warm ___ front   cold ___ front   stationary ___ front   occluded ___ front

WORD BANK

warm air mass   cold air mass   cold front
warm front   stationary front occluded front

A Cold Front

Name_____

The illustration below is a front between two air masses. The cooler air mass is replacing the warmer air mass.

Label the cloud types associated with the cold front pictured below.

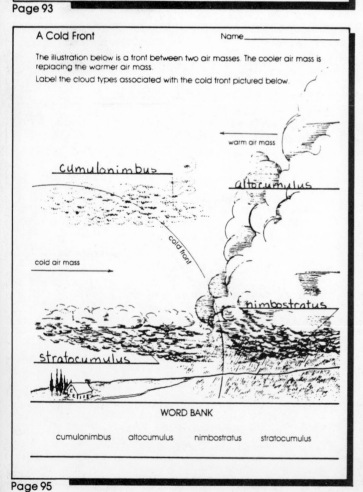

WORD BANK

cumulonimbus   altocumulus   nimbostratus   stratocumulus

A Warm Front

Name_____

The illustration below is a front between two air masses. A warm air mass is pushing a cold air mass.

Label the cloud types associated with the warm front pictured below.

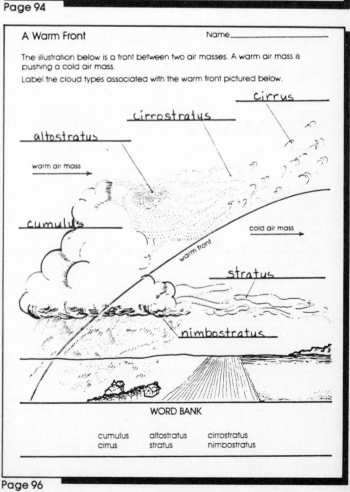

WORD BANK

cumulus   altostratus   cirrostratus
cirrus   stratus   nimbostratus

Answer Key

Cloud Types

Name _____

Label the cloud types pictured below.

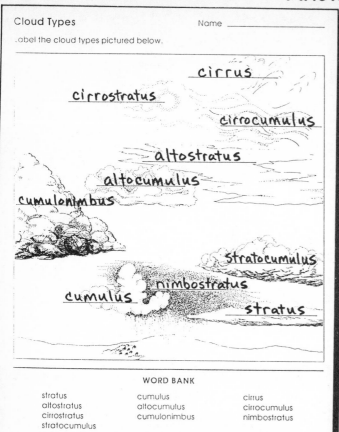

cirrus
cirrostratus
cirrocumulus
altostratus
altocumulus
cumulonimbus
stratocumulus
nimbostratus
cumulus
stratus

WORD BANK

stratus	cumulus	cirrus
altostratus	altocumulus	cirrocumulus
cirrostratus	cumulonimbus	nimbostratus
stratocumulus		

Clouds and Weather

Name _____

Different types of clouds are often associated with a specific kind of weather. Four different kinds of clouds are pictured below. Write the name of the cloud type, a description of the cloud, and the kind of weather associated with each one.

Cloud Type	Name	Description	Associated Weather
	cumulus	piles of "puffy" clouds	fair, sometimes showers
	cumulo-nimbus	tall, dark and billowing	thunderstorms
	stratus	smooth sheets, or layers	steady drizzle
	cirrus	thin, wispy clouds	fair

WORD BANK

thunderstorms	cumulonimbus	cumulus
fair, sometimes showers	thin, wispy clouds	stratus
steady drizzle	tall, dark and billowing	fair
smooth sheets, or layers	piles of "puffy" clouds	cirrus

Tomorrow's Weather Forecast

Name _____

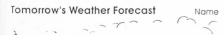

Check the accuracy of the weather forecasts in your area for the next week. Complete the chart by writing the forecast for "tomorrow's" weather and then recording the actual weather for that day. Indicate whether or not the forecast was accurate by circling yes or no.

	Date	Temp. Range	Precipi-tation	Wind Speed	Wind Direction	Sky Condition	Accurate Forecast? (Circle.)
Forecast							Yes
Actual							No
Forecast							Yes
Actual							No
Forecast							Yes
Actual							No
Forecast							Yes
Actual							No
Forecast							Yes
Actual							No
Forecast							Yes
Actual							No
Forecast							Yes
Actual							No
Forecast							Yes
Actual							No

Weather Tools

Name _____

Meteorologists use many instruments to gather their data. Label each of these weather instruments.

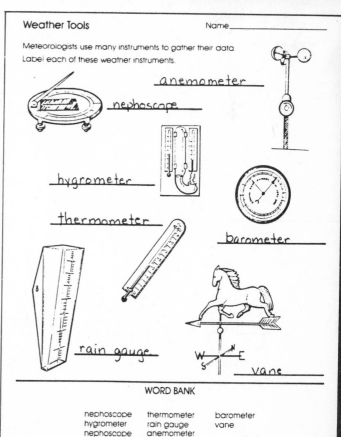

anemometer
nephoscope
hygrometer
thermometer
barometer
rain gauge
vane

WORD BANK

nephoscope	thermometer	barometer
hygrometer	rain gauge	vane
nephoscope	anemometer	

Answer Key

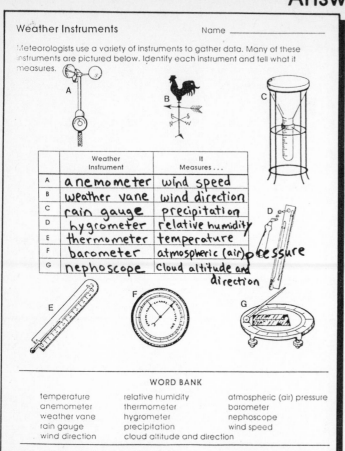

Weather Instruments

Name _____

Meteorologists use a variety of instruments to gather data. Many of these instruments are pictured below. Identify each instrument and tell what it measures.

	Weather Instrument	It Measures...
A	anemometer	wind speed
B	weather vane	wind direction
C	rain gauge	precipitation
D	hygrometer	relative humidity
E	thermometer	temperature
F	barometer	atmospheric (air) pressure
G	nephoscope	Cloud altitude and direction

WORD BANK

temperature	relative humidity	atmospheric (air) pressure
anemometer	thermometer	barometer
weather vane	hygrometer	nephoscope
rain gauge	precipitation	wind speed
wind direction	cloud altitude and direction	

Page 101

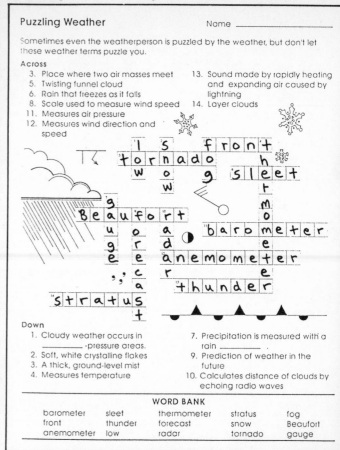

Puzzling Weather

Name _____

Sometimes even the weatherperson is puzzled by the weather, but don't let these weather terms puzzle you.

Across

3. Place where two air masses meet
5. Twisting funnel cloud
6. Rain that freezes as it falls
8. Scale used to measure wind speed
11. Measures air pressure
12. Measures wind direction and speed
13. Sound made by rapidly heating and expanding air caused by lightning
14. Layer clouds

Down

1. Cloudy weather occurs in _____ -pressure areas.
2. Soft, white crystalline flakes
3. A thick, ground-level mist
4. Measures temperature
7. Precipitation is measured with a rain _____
9. Prediction of weather in the future
10. Calculates distance of clouds by echoing radio waves

WORD BANK

barometer	sleet	thermometer	stratus	fog
front	thunder	forecast	snow	Beaufort
anemometer	low	radar	tornado	gauge

Page 102